Cardboard Confessionals

Mitch Reed

Special thank you to the printing company that brought you
Cardboard Confessionals:
Randy Lesnar
Western Commercial Printing
4005 South Western Ave.
P.O. Box 5184
Sioux Falls South Dakota 57117-5184

Resources:
Huffington Post
Center of Disease Control
TED Talks: Ric Elias
TED Talks: Candy Chang

Editor: Nora Groft

Design: Shari Reed

Special Contributors: 2016-2017 WSS Sociology Class, VJ Smith, Misty Comes, Nic Ahmann, Nancy Adair, Brett Brennan, Julie Kneeland, Becky Schlotterbeck, John Melius, Kara VerWey

ISBN: 978-0-092-99723-9

Printed in the United States of America

cardboard
confessionals

With any questions, comments, stories, or inquires please email me or contact me on twitter at:

cardboardconfessionals@gmail.com

@mireed20

Table of Contents

Preface

When I was a sophomore in high school, I decided I needed to work in the educational field. Undecided in the subject area, I knew I wanted to be in a school. I had a memorable school experience at Northwestern School in Mellette, South Dakota. In my early years in the education profession at Waverly-South Shore and Deubrook Elementary School, I made a lot of comparisons. I looked at the differences and similarities of the teachers, students, classes, and activities. If I would have had the insight I have now on how a school functions and the importance of education, I believe I would not have taken my school experience as lightly as I did. I think back on some of my peers and how I could have changed their school experience by just including them and showing them that I cared about them and their well-being; that is all that some people need to be successful. As I have aged, I also have learned how our viewpoints and priorities change.

Everyone should take the time to reminisce on their experiences and values. Writing a book requires one to do this. People can reevaluate the actions that they have taken in life; they can examine the relationships that they have made. This writing process has encouraged me to reach out to people with whom I have lost touch. While writing this, I have reinforced the passion that I have for the people in my life as well as my occupation.

There will be concepts throughout the book to which teachers and students will be able to relate. Those who are not in the educational field will have their eyes opened to some of the issues, dreams, aspirations, and thoughts of students in society today. The pages include dialogue on my experience that I have encountered during my time in the classroom and in education.

Life is short; passion and relationships are the true key to happiness, and observing a wide range of experiences makes for the best life. This book will help readers to take a step back and look at the relationships in their lives and how they can improve them. I hope that readers can see the power that they have to change people's days, weeks, years, or even life with the simple conversations and words you use. We can empower people each day to strive to be better, leading to a fulfilling life for ourselves as well. Understanding the professed and concealed issues of society's youth stands as the first step in helping them solve these problems.

At 24 years old, I received my first administration job. The idea of working with students and leading a staff excited me. Imagine a young kid who wanted to conquer the world; that was me. As my years went on, the process started to slow down. The excitement of the job dwindled. I often asked myself how I could bring the excitement back. I realized very quickly that excitement leaves and may not come back. My excitement had turned into passion; passion for my job, passion for the people around me, and passion for the future of the school. My passion included my family within the school. My wife worked as the Title I teacher in the district, and my 1-year-old daughter became known as the "community baby," getting passed around at all of the school and community events. I loved it at Waverly-South Shore School. The students strived, the staff cared, and the community supported. The people who have surrounded me throughout my life have helped me build passion. After moving to Deubrook, I began to realize the importance of education and the teachers. They are on the front lines with students, battling various problem that arise. The teachers at Deubrook are committed to excellence, and it drove me to be not only a better educator but also a better person.

As soon as that excitement turned to passion, I started to cherish every day, especially in the school building. I began to take in everything and realized that life is too short to sweat the small issues. Students and their lives became fascinating. Why were students acting the way they did? How much influence does home life have on a student's achievement? Will they be prepared for the life after high school? How can I get students to understand that what they do with their time is important? These questions and that type of mindset drove me to continue to build strong relationships with the people around me, including the students.

To fully understand students and their thoughts, sometimes we need to get to their level. When I was in school, time meant nothing. Anything significant that happened in our lives, we simply swept under the rug; we lived in the moment, and no one was going to stop us. We enjoyed life and created many memories, but I often think we didn't embrace them like we should have. I heard many times from our high school football coach to embrace the moment and never take it for granted. This never really made sense to me until I got into college and the real world started making a little more sense.

How do we as educators get students to understand that what they do in high school matters? The relationships they make, the impressions they leave, the experiences they encounter, and the morals they develop play a significant role in their success later in life. I didn't want to be the teacher or administrator who jumps up on his soap box and talks philosophically to these students, but I wanted them to understand that if they are spending time doing something, it matters. Time is valuable and full-hearted attention needs to be given to the task at hand. Adolescents and young adults especially need to understand they will never get time spent in their youth back. Some of the best advice I received growing up was:

"Don't look back on your life and regret time not spent well."

People with children in school know that when their students started school, the family dynamics changed, and school became an important part of the familial identity. When students come home, they are asked how school was. When they are eating dinner, they are asked what they learn. Families that put importance in education give their students a better chance of succeeding later in life. Everything I have learned has been in a school setting. I learned manners in elementary, awkwardness in middle school, responsibility and direction in high school, accountability in college, and passion in my professional career. So many of my values and viewpoints developed in an educational setting, and I would like to thank all my prior teachers, classmates, coworkers, and students for my strong foundation.

They always say the best way to learn is to make a connection to the information being presented. My experiences have reinforced my passion. The people one meets throughout life will mold their values and passions; that is why it is important to surround oneself with good people. I have been fortunate enough to learn from some great people. These people showed me that life is too short; the importance of being supportive and caring means everything, and that anyone can change people's day with just a smile. A few lessons I have learned have come from people who are no longer with us. These people lived with passion, their lives spent focusing on the big picture. They lived in the moment while setting goals to be successful in the future. Their demeanor is what I admired most about them.

I have taken what I learned from these people and tried to implement that into my life. How can I make things better for my family? How can I help and impact the lives of people whom I encounter? What can I pass on to them to help them achieve their goals? How do I leave a legacy behind of which my family can be proud? Those are questions to which I will continue to seek the answers. Those questions drive people. Those questions that, when answered, bring fulfillment to one's life. I will continue to search for those answers and rely on the people I love and the people I meet to help me get to where I want to be.

Many people have helped me along the way. My wife and daughter have fueled my passion for life and push me to be a better person each and every day. My parents and family have been supportive throughout my life, including this process. I could not have completed this project without the students in my sociology class who gave this project purpose. A special thanks to Misty Comes, Nic Ahmann, Nancy Adair, Becky Schlotterbeck, Julie Kneeland, John Melius, and Brett Brennan on reading bits and pieces throughout the process and giving me constructive criticism. I appreciate V.J. Smith and his guidance throughout the book writing, editing, and publishing process. Lastly, I want to thank my editor Nora Groft for her hard work and dedication to help this project be successful. Without them, the completion of this project would have been a massive undertaking.

Foreword

Have you ever asked yourself why? Why do people do the things they do? Why do situations turn out the way they do? Why is life so difficult? I used to ask myself these questions all the time until I met Mr. Mitch Reed. Little did I know that when I met this guy five years ago, he would change my outlook on life, and help me to become a better educator, parent, and person. I started teaching with Mitch in 2012. I was new to the school and was beginning my twelfth year of teaching. Mitch was starting out his career as a high school teacher. He pushed to change the world with all his great ideas and wasn't going to let anything get in his way. Interestingly, he did everything he said he was going to do, and was very successful along his journey. It took him three years in education to work up to the principal position. He was not only the guy to go to at school, but also was visible to students, staff, and the community. He went to every school function and showed the students and community he cared.

My daughter was diagnosed with autism in 2015 at the age of ten. I always thought she may have it, but doctors always told me no. Imagine the devastation when a team of highly qualified doctors told me my thoughts were true: I was inconsolable. I told Mr. Reed the diagnosis, and he was empathetic, but he also said the news did not change who she is. We have all grown to love her and that won't change because of the diagnosis. The diagnosis was just a label on the things that she does differently; it doesn't change or define her.

My daughter had a serious infatuation with Mitch. Anytime she saw him at school, she would have to be with him. He always made her feel important and took time for her. It's people like Mitch who truly make a difference in the lives of children. He would even come over to our house, sit in the hot garage, and color with her. How many twenty-something-year-old males would do this? He has become a great friend to my family and I appreciate his influence in our life.

In this book, he will provide insight to help us become a better people. He takes bad situations and is somehow able to turn them into learning opportunities. Our success can be determined in how we look at the situations in our life. His wisdom at such a young age is admirable. The way he connected with his students is truly amazing. He explains the importance of knowing people and their situations before judging or dubbing them as 'bad.' That is truly important for educators. We can help people by understanding their situations and showing them we care can make all the difference in the world. I highly recommend this book, and I know it will change your life in some way or another. The insight he has shown through his words is insurmountable and life changing. I will never forget one quote Mitch would always say whenever you asked him how he was, he would say "I'm living the dream," and I truly believe him when he says that. Let him help you to live your dream or do it a little better.

Misty Comes

Elementary Educator

Introduction

In our daily life, we fall into the trap of going through the motions. This may inhibit us from taking advantage of special people or opportunities around us. Who would have known a class project would change the lives of seven students and their teacher? These seven students with different backgrounds all left my sociology class periods with a clearer, deeper understanding of what their peers encounter socially and emotionally on a daily basis. Our project opened them to appreciate the courage and strength of their peers and allowed those students to look at themselves in a different way, helping them consider and share their accomplishments, goals, and innermost thoughts. Some excerpts in this book are deep, and I hope these students received a release through this project that allowed them to ease some of the pain in their life and take some of the weight off of their shoulders.

The project consisted of middle school and high school students anonymously answering a series of seven questions, considered and chosen by my sociology class.

Those questions included the following:
1. What is one thing you want to do before you die?
2. What makes a meaningful life?
3. On what one thing in life you have given up?
4. What is something that people misunderstand about you?
5. Of what are you most proud?
6. What do you think about when you are alone?
7. Describe your life in six words.

When students answered the daily question, they deposited their response in a cardboard box during the lunch hour. I appreciated the seriousness the students put into this project. They talked about what they wrote afterward with their friends and the rest of the students at lunch table. This experience got students thinking about the future and their role in changing it for the better. Although some of the confessions we received were a bit farfetched, some were achievable, and writing it down proved to be the first step to achieving.

At any school, students interact fairly regularly with dozens of their peers, especially at a small, rural school like Waverly-South Shore. And though they may have a great deal of superficial knowledge about each other as a consequence of growing up together, they often have a much more shallow knowledge of each other personally. This project forced students to take a deeper look into the unknown and appreciate what makes people unique. Their past experiences and the memories they have developed from those experiences make them who they are today. Growing up, kids do not have all the control over what they experience, so taking that into consideration is important when building relationships.

As our class continued to talk about the findings of "Cardboard Confessionals," I began to see a change in the sociology students and began to see them reminisce about experiences they have encountered in school and their personal life. When educators get students to take a step back and reflect, we see meaningful conversations that promote critical thinking. We start to see concepts in the world make sense to these students, and questions begin to flow. Throughout the project, I heard great questions that challenged the status quo and it made them question some of the norms to which they are accustomed.

At the end of the day, if we can get not only students, but also adults to understand the power they have and that every relationship they build is valuable, we have made a difference. After this project, our students became a bit more cognizant of the feelings and backgrounds of the people around them and realized they do have the ability to change another person's day. When we talked about making a difference, I had these seven students pull out a note card and write a thank you to someone in the building who has made a difference in their life. Some of the students took ten minutes to write this thank you. After they completed the task, I asked them how long it would take them to write a note card full of displeasures and upsetting situations in their life. A moment of silence then occurred. Some of them realized they would have had more than a notecard in ten minutes of writing. I then told students the more we practice being positive and begin to recognize those who make a difference in our lives, the smaller our problems become. The more we practice being negative, the larger our problems become. These lessons change the mindset of students and hopefully that spreads through the people they touch throughout the day.

These students bought into the fact that this project is more than just a typical school project; it instilled a sense of power into each one of them. They began to understand the influence they had. They pushed others to be truthful and made the classroom a place where they can be honest. They grasped that people need a place to release information bothering them, and unloading withheld information may help them throughout the day. I hope the students in our sociology class can come back years after graduating and talk about that class and the significance it has played in their life. After all, a major dream of an educator is to hear about a memory made in our presences that impacted past student's lives.

Chapter 1

Setting the Stage

This project stemmed from a wall constructed in Brookings, South Dakota. On the wall, it stated, "Before I die, I want to..." The wall had white lines printed under this statement for people to write their answers with sidewalk chalk. I began to think about how everyone who wrote on that wall had a story, a story that deserved to be shared and a journey worth being celebrated. On the wall listed a wide range of dreams and desires that displayed a sense of safety and security. This list included:

· Travel the world

· Be a great mom

· Change lives

· Make my first million

· Live my life the way I want to live it

I went home and did some more research on this "wall." The story proved much more extensive than I realized. A woman by the name of Candy Chang came up with the idea in New Orleans. She wanted to spruce up the neighborhood and leave a positive impact on the city. Her idea spread through seventy countries around the world. I watched her TED Talk and wondered how I could implement a similar impact in my classroom.[1]

I decided I wanted to know the stories of our students at Waverly-South Shore. Not only did I want to know them, but also I wanted to provide an outlet for them to share any thoughts that might take some weight off their shoulders. The first step in this process meant generating the questions. I had my students generate questions we felt would help us get to know our student body more deeply.

---

[1] Chang, Candy. "Before I Die I Want To." TED Talks. TED Global 2012, Nov. 2012.

Students spent the lunch period thinking about how they were going to answer the prompt. The Sociology class decided to use a simple cardboard box as a depository. I placed the questions, written on small strips of paper, and pens at each lunch table for the students. Many students felt the weight come off their shoulders every time they responded to a prompt. After the project, I had a student come up and tell me it was the only time she could be true to herself throughout the day. I had students come up to me and ask about the question of the day or what the question was going to be the following day. As the project accelerated, we began to see students look forward to this part of the day. After lunch, I compiled the answers into a spreadsheet to avoid any handwriting recognition that would compromise the anonymity that we felt necessary.

If we wanted to make this project successful inside the classroom, we had to get to know each other personally. To accomplish this, we each wrote a short biography to help explain why we might tend toward certain opinions or reactions. This activity allowed each student to appreciate each other's journeys.

I came from a two-parent household with a good amount of support; however, when my parents were gone, I had to step up and take care of some of the things within the household. I learned a lot growing up and believe that is why I am in education. My past has given me a different perspective in education and in life in general. I have a great respect for my parents and still have a great relationship with them. What they have done for me has made me who I am today.

Our sociology class was dynamic. The experiences these students endured were diverse and fueled the conversations within the classroom. The reason this class was successful was the trust that was built. They felt comfortable to share their thoughts, dreams, fears, and aspirations.

One class member was a foreign-exchange student from Spain. He came from a working-class family in a suburb of Madrid. Growing up, the economy endured crisis that hit his family pretty hard. He needed to grow up quickly. He knew education was the one way to help him excel in life. He understood from an early age that nobody owed him anything and if he wanted something, he had to work hard to get it. He lives with the philosophy that excuses get him nowhere, and family is important when dealing with crisis. It is important to enjoy life rather than let it pass by. He hopes when he gets older he can leave this world knowing there was nothing left for him to do.

Another class member resided on her family farm and has been there her entire life. She has one little brother and an older sister to whom she is very close. Her parents are very loving and their support means a lot to her. Her relationship with family and friends and her experiences she encountered have made her who she is today. She plans on using that support from those close to her to help her succeed in the future.

Another class member was also raised on a farm. She has been around animals all her life. School is something at which she works extremely hard, and she has earned everything she has achieved. She is involved in many activities throughout school and has met a lot of different people. Some people whom she looks up to have passed, and they have taught her strong values and made her appreciate the time she has with loved ones.

One resided in a small town as the youngest of four boys. He is close to his brothers, and they have driven him to be successful. They all have gone on to college, and he hopes one day he can as well. Things in his life have not come easily, so he has to work hard to achieve highly. At the age of 12, his parents divorced, and he stays with his mom. He still communicates with his dad and tries to strengthen their relationship as well.

Another student has grandparents who took her in when she was about three, as her mother did not have the financial or emotional support to raise her properly. Her dad battles with alcoholism and can't function properly to support himself, let alone a child. Growing up in a small town on a Native American reservation, she felt great support from those around her. Her grandparents were the ideal grandparents; they supported her. As she got older, she struggled to understand why she was not with her parents and became insecure and felt unwanted. Her drop of self-esteem led to a path of substance abuse that took a toll on her life. She was sent to treatment then moved in with her mom. Not even nine months later, she and her siblings were put into foster care. After two homes, they finally found a good fit, but they had to fight to stay there due to social service regulations. In the end, the tribal government saw that the families they were with were best for the children so they were able to stay; they are currently with those families today. Her journey impacts her but does not define her.

One of the girls who was in the class has one older sister, one younger brother, and a younger sister. She also has one older step-brother and two younger step-sisters. When looking at her childhood, she lived a pretty average life. In second grade, things became different; her grandpa passed away. Then she and her family went to live with her grandma to help with tasks around the house. After a few months, her mom moved back to town with her older sister. At the end of second grade, her mom moved back in with them. Life was normal again, at least until her little sister was born. She developed normally for the first couple of years until she ended up in the hospital for just over a week. She lost many of her abilities, and to this day, she needs help with just about everything. After that, they learned that she had autism. Life has changed drastically for the family since the sister's birth, but the family agrees it is one of the best things that has happened to them. During the summer of her freshman year, her parents split up. At the end of summer the following year, her mom got remarried. She respects her parents and their ability to put their differences aside for the good of their children. Her life has been difficult at times, but she wouldn't want it any other way.

The last student grew up on a small farm in South Dakota with her mom, dad, and younger sister. Growing up on a farm and having supportive parents created her passion for agriculture and striving to be the best she could be. School comes easily to her, but she continues to work hard. Her goal is to give back and share her knowledge with others in order to make a difference in life. She is known as a caring person, which makes her passionate about the concerns of other people during this sociology experiment. She learned a lot through this project, and it has changed her perspective on life and the people around her.

TALK TO HIM GO TO CANADA GO TO ... GO TO EUROPE LOVE ... SAVE A ...
DEAD 300 MPH HAVE MONEY ... GET MARRIED AND HAVE KIDS GO TO HAWAII HAVE MY DREAM JOB
SEE JOSH TURNER IN CONCERT ... GO TO HAWAII HAVE MY DREAM JOB
DEEP SEA FISHING ... ROD WRITE A SONG FOR SOMEONE I LOVE
... A GOOD LIFE LIVE ON THE LAKE ... HANG OUT WITH TOM FELTON AND DANIEL RADCLIFF ...
GO TO WEST POINT SKY DIVE
MANSION

What is one thing you want to do before you die?

O CANADA
BE A PRO FO... ? BRONC... OUT GAINING WEIGHT BECAUSE ...
A LIFE GO A DAY WITH... O TO DISNEY WORLD
TO THE MASTER... VISIT ALL 50 STATES LIVE
...NDS AGAIN ... IN NEW YORK CITY
EE MY INTE... CLIFF DIVING ...
EP SEA FISH... TELL IM I AM SORRY
GO TO THE EMPIRE STATE BU... ... BE A PRO FOOTBALL PLAYER LIVE A GOOD LIFE
LOVE SOMEONE SKY DIVE E ON THE LAKE HAVE 1000 BABIES
LL HER HOW I REALLY FEEL WANT TO GO SEE THE TITANIC
A DAY WITHOUT WANTING TO DIE LOVE SORRY ...AND HAVE I KID AND ADOPT I KID OUT AND POO
LIVE DEEP SEA FISHING NOT BE D... ...D HAVE KIDS FISH AND HUNT LIVE MY LIFE TO THE FULLEST
TO TO A DENVER BRONCOS GAME ... GO TO EUROPE
E MONEY GET MAR... ...ED TELL IM I AM SORRY
SIT GERMANY HE... ...ED STATES ONCE
GO BAC...
ET A JOB JUMP... ...T AN AIRPLANE LEAVE GO IN A SUBMARINE SKY DIVE
ROW DEEPER IN MY FAITH SEE MY INTERNET FRIENDS AGAIN GO 300 MPH GO TO IRELAND
A MANSION VISIT GERMANY BUILD A DREAM HOUSE GO TO IRELAND CURE CANCER
WRITE A SONG FOR SOMEONE I LOVE CLIFF DIVING
HANG OUT WITH TOM FELTON AND DANIEL RADCLIFF
ET A CAR RACE IN THE X GAMES GO TO THE EMPIRE STATE BUILDING IN NEW YORK CITY LIVE A GOOD LIFE
DIVE LIFE GO 300 MPH ... GO TO ALASKA
VE A LOVING FAMILY GO TO DISNEY WORLD GO TO DUKE UNC GAME EAT LUNCH
VISIT ALL 50 STATES VISIT THE ROMAN COLESIUM EAT LUNCH GO IN A SUBMARINE
CHANGE PEOPLES LIVES IN A POSITIVE WAY HAVE 1000 BABIES VISIT GERMANY
GO TO DISNEY WORLD HAVE 1000 BABIES
GO TO WEST POINT CURE CANCER GO TO HAWAII

The first prompt given to the Waverly-South Shore student body received a phenomenal response. Who would have thought that looking at a mural, inspired by Candy Chang, in Brookings, South Dakota, on a Sunday afternoon would change the way students thought about the people around them? This project also changed the way people communicated with one another. They no longer hesitated to have tough conversations with those around them because they knew those conversations could help them down the road. Students strived to build strong relationships.

Seventy-five students answered, "What is one thing you want to do before you die" and some of those answers blew my mind. Some of the answers I found interesting included the following: to visit the Roman Coliseum, cure cancer, help as many people as I can, see the Titanic, see my Internet friends, cliff dive, and go back to where my ancestors lived. My first thought when reading most of these confessions was how similar they are to what adults would fill out. This is why education is one of the most rewarding professions. We get to help students mold their futures and dreams. Reading these confessions shed light on our students. Observing people's dreams and aspirations through this project was inspiring.

Although we are in a small community, our students' desires vary. I chose these seven confessions as an example of the variety and dynamics of our small student population.

Save a life

First off, how cool are kids? A middle or high school student came up with this? I went into education wanting to help students and to change their lives for the better, but they have done it for me. As an educator, the best class we can have is a class that teaches the educator just as much as the educator teaches the students.

When I read this confessional to the class, save a life, silence struck. My students began to consider the worth of that kind of aspiration. The fragile state of life isn't often at the forefront of our minds. I saw students shake their heads and appreciate the significance of saving a life.

In education, we tend to focus on the things students cannot do well and often forget all the things that make them awesome. Students walk through the halls wanting to save lives, not win a million dollars, not travel to every country, not marry a supermodel, but to save lives. This type of response reassures us in regards to the future and what this generation can bring to the table.

When people focus on the good in life, the more they find along the way. Expectations are set for people when others see the good in them and they try their best to meet those expectations. Perhaps the student who wrote this confession had someone in his or her life that changed them, possibly even saved their life. Those who have been graced with caring people in their life obtain a clearer vision of their purpose. Many obstacles blur the true purpose of one's life. Being "saved" allows people to look back on their past and put it into perspective.

We talked about what different ways a life can be saved. The first examples shared included administering CPR to someone in need, pulling someone out of a burning house, and using the Heimlich maneuver. All are great examples of how one can save a life. The initial discussion clearly focused on physical life-saving procedures. I then asked for the definition of "saving a life." Is saving a life only keeping another person alive when they may otherwise perish? Could we consider helping people make good life decisions to be saving a life? We agreed that saving a life encompasses much more than strictly keeping someone alive. We then talked about if they had witnessed a life being saved.

Here is one of the stories that I shared:

In my short life, I have seen a few instances of the power of people changing others' lives. My grandpa would make people's day by the way he greeted them and cared for them. The way he asked strangers how they were doing was sincere, and I admired his ability to do that. Regardless of the background or the experiences, he wanted to help them succeed. He received satisfaction by welcoming people into his life, helping people to accept who they are, and pushing them to be the best version of themselves.

I knew he had saved lives when he passed away. The tears that were shed at his funeral were a testament to the lives he touched.

While my grandpa was receiving hospice care in his house a few short days before he passed, he received a letter from a student whom he had forty years prior. My grandpa taught math and later became a school administrator. As I watched my grandpa read the letter, I witnessed him cry for the first time in my life. This written evidence of the good he did in another person's life put my grandpa's soul at peace in his final days. At that moment, he had realized the power he had and that he had "saved lives" along the way. For a man who sacrificed so much for others, I was happy to see him receive such a meaningful gift.

People have the opportunity to serve in many different roles. My grandpa showed all of us the influence we have on people and how we can help. We are all put in situations where we can make positive change. We have the ability to support, give guidance, and influence the people around us. When we set out on a given day, we need to understand the power we have to help people for the better. The people who understand and take advantage of these opportunities, or better yet, search for these opportunities, have the potential to save lives.

<u>Student Comment</u>
I think if one of the things a person wants to do before you die is to be able to help someone else live, it really says a lot of that person.

Talk to him one last time

After reading this confessional, a lot of questions came to my mind. What was the last conversation like between the person who wrote this and "him?" Was it meaningful? Were they upset? Were comments left unsaid? How much can one conversation change the lives of people? Has the man passed away or just passed out of this student's life?

This man must have played a significant role in this student's life. Could talking to this person one last time change this student? Would his or her memories change of this person if he or she could speak to him again? Has losing this person changed the way this student builds relationships? Opportunities are presented to us in many different ways, and it is how we take advantage of those opportunities that defines our success.

This project set out to help the students understand people and their experiences that affect them in many different ways. If anything, this project could help these seven students build patience with the people around them and open their eyes to the misfortune of their peers. This may help them begin to appreciate what they have. This confession helped the students in our class understand the importance of meaningful communication and embracing the moment.

After the students began to think on a national level, we began to look at stories in the news about suicide, murder, and other tragic events. We began to put ourselves in the shoes of those involved. The first event discussed among the class was September 11th. So many people were lost tragically on that day. Many words were left unspoken, and the people who were left behind feel empty because of that lack of closure.

Sincerity tends to be lost when we get into a routine. We begin to take opportunities and people around us for granted.

Sadly, most of the time, it takes tragic events or misfortune to help put perspective in our life. When I was young, my main priority at holidays was eating as much as I could and watching TV. This was a common trend until we lost an uncle tragically to a heart attack when I was a sophomore. I looked back on our relationship and regret the wasted time I missed with him. He was a great man, and I didn't take the time to appreciate him and his efforts to be a good role model to his family. After his death, our family gatherings changed for the better. We took the time to ask questions and to show those in our family we cared for one another. Since that time, I can say I have taken the time to engage myself in more meaningful conversations with my relatives.

A few years ago, when I was coaching baseball, a player's father died in a tragic car accident. I received news from his son through a text message hours after it happened. He said he was not going to be able to make the baseball game that day. The news was shocking. The family was left searching for answers. They put their faith in God to take care of them through tough times. They used their tribulations as a test and came out stronger than ever. Before he left this world, this father had built a foundation of faith in God. Their faith and ability to stay strong during tough times can be a valuable lesson from which many families can benefit. I think about a man of his respect and dignity and what his last words would be to his loved ones. His message would be full of hope, faith, and inspiration that would help fuel those around him to live better lives.

From my experiences with people I know, I have learned that "see you later" is not guaranteed. We can learn something from each person we meet. As our relationship grows, so does our knowledge of various concepts. From my uncle, I learned that life is as stressful as we make it. From the baseball father, I learned that love and faith will conquer all. Every conversation we have with people provides an opportunity to grow relationships and develop personally.

Student Comment

I can relate to this post because I lost my great-grandpa last October, and he was really involved with our family. I would do anything to talk with him one more time about World War II and his role.

Love someone

To make high school students uncomfortable, ask them the definition of love. The interesting part about love is the power it has over people, or how the lack of love affects people. It is not until we lose a loving relationship until we understand the importance of love in our life. We all have needs, and those needs are different. Some people use love to drive them to achieve great milestones. Others struggle to see that love and it pushes them to make bad decisions in certain situations. The absence of love in life is one of the biggest deterrents in our world. Without love, passion in our relationships is hard to come by. A gratifying accomplishment having people to love and share our successes with.

I am curious what made this student write this on his or her confessional. Is this student part of a family who is loving and aspires to have that same sort of love when he or she gets older? Is this a situation where this student feels neglected at home and sees loving relationships around him or her? All students deserve a loving environment at home. They deserve the opportunity to come home and brag about getting the lead in the all-school play, acing a test, winning the game, or making the honor roll. They deserve the comfort and support after encountering disappointment throughout childhood and adolescence. Unfortunately, not all students have that fortune. The presence or absence of this person plays a role in our development as well.

When talking to happy people and asking them where they see themselves in five to ten years, the word love tends to pop up. A majority of the time, the feeling consists of having a loving family or a good relationship with God. To have a fulfilling life, people need love in their lives in one shape or form.

In American society, love is a word used often but not always fully understood. Everyone is graced with opportunities to love. Unfortunately, challenges and obstacles that we face can complicate these opportunities, and some people endure more complications than others. For these people, finding loving relationships and working to flourish these relationships can prove more difficult.

Without love, happiness eludes those searching for it. People who experience true happiness are the ones who open themselves up to loving with all their hearts and allow others to return that feeling. We struggle to put ourselves out there because we are afraid of being hurt. People come from many backgrounds where pain and agony occurs frequently. Opening up to people after being hurt so many times can be difficult, but it is essential.

With loving relationships in students' lives, learning becomes much more achievable for the various students in a school. They rely on their relationships to take risks in the classroom and know they have support if something were to go wrong. Love comes in many different ways, but the love we see in schools is necessary for student success. Unconditional love encourages students to try their best and to find their identity. The most influential teachers are those who relate to the students and show them they care about their well-being and are invested in their future.

In education, we see many students walk through our halls. We encourage them to open up to new experiences and opportunities when they are conditioned to do the opposite. We try to give these students a safe environment as we help them make sense of their experiences. The best teachers seek students who need support and work with them to be successful. That sort of expectation cannot be laid out in a job description, but the ones who take the extra step are those who care about students and went into the profession for the right reasons. These types of relationships at school can help make up for, though certainly never replace, a lack of loving relationships in other areas of our students' lives.

Live a good life

What makes for a good life? That is the first question asked when this confession was read to the class. The feedback from the students was enlightening. Out of the students in the class, everyone had a different description for a good life. Some of the students mentioned having a loving family, others mentioned succeeding in their work, some said being devout in their religion, and others said being healthy. Some people are very simple in what they want, others require extensive demands to consider their lives "good."

I had my class write down five items they needed to accomplish a good life; then the lesson truly began. We began to discuss the process of how to fulfill each of their "goals." Even the students who had similar goals varied distinctly in their criteria for accomplishment. I had two students list a successful job as a component in obtaining a good life. I asked them to include their measure of a successful job. One wanted security and good people with whom to work. The other student stated he wanted to make a good wage.

Even though our goals we set for ourselves may be the same, the route we take to get there is completely different.

The choices we make throughout the journey help define us and solidify our character. For some, the route may be much more difficult, but wouldn't that make the accomplishment even more meaningful? Our job as educators is to help our students on their path and give them every tool needed to be successful. For some students, we may need to guide them every step of the way. For other students, letting them know we believe in them may be all it takes.

The conversation changed as we began discussing how backgrounds and upbringing played a role in what was needed to live a good life. Does one have a different outlook on life based on where they grew up? Does it change based on how much money their parents made? Does it change depending on religion or gender?

Everyone is dealt a hand in life; it is just we play our cards that writes our story.

When I think of people living a good life, I think of my parents. They are two people who enjoy spending time together and engaging in new experiences. As long as they are spending time together, no time is wasted. Before they met, they have stories that shape who they are, and they wouldn't change that. They have expanded their experiences since my sisters and I have left the house. I appreciate what they have done for my life, but what I appreciate more is how they have taught me to live life. They are not perfect by any means, but they are a significant reason on why I am who I am.

I learned from my parents that no time spent are on earth is insignificant, and it is never too late to make changes for the better. They live life open to change and realized that any experience can be one to change their lives. They fed off one another for happiness; an attribute crucial for a happy marriage. They focused their life on the relationships they had built. What was more inspiring was not just the relationships but how they maintained them. They never told people they cared, they showed it. My parents show people their happiness by the way they treat others day to day. This is how I know my parents live a good life.

Going one day without wanting to die

Reading this confession is shocking and heartbreaking regardless of the age group or situation of the person. It maybe even more shocking because this was observed in a school. When I read it to the class, they had mixed feelings. Some were very nervous about the statement while others understood the feelings being addressed. Some of the classmates never knew anyone who had committed or attempted suicide, while one of the students had a close friend who had committed suicide and she got a little emotional during the class. The dynamic of the students' experiences made this topic challenging. One of the students stated that suicide was a selfish act; some agreed, others strongly disagreed. Through this discussion, I became mediator and posed questions for students to contemplate and discuss.

It was conversations like these that helped people to open up more in their confessions. They began to believe in the process and saw the positive aspects involved. They began to see the impact they can make on the people around them with just showing them they care. When people feel a sense of comfort and security, they are more likely to open up and share, both the good and the bad aspects. Students were beginning to receive an emotional release by sharing their secrets, ambitions, and dreams. This gave them a sense of safety and security.

What was this individual going through each day that made him or her write this confession? Was home life a battle every day? Was something from the past so insurmountable it couldn't be overcome? Did he or she struggle to fit in at school and couldn't find a better alternative?

According to the Center of Disease Control in 2015, 17 percent of students seriously considered suicide and 8 percent of those teens have attempted suicide.[2] People encounter hurtful experiences each and every day. Regardless of this knowledge, we still struggle to give some students the support needed. These students are going through tough times and are still developing. That combination leads to various mental issues. Another aspect that fuels these mental issues are the expectations placed on these students from parents, friends, school, and society. When they are not able

---

[2] *Suicide: Facts at a Glance*. Center of Disease and Control, www.cdc.gov/violenceprevention/pdf/suicide-datasheet-a.pdf.

to live up to these standards, people see them as weak and inferior. These situations build up and can be too much for students to hurdle.

I asked the class how we can help people struggling with emotional issues to see the light in situations. I continued by saying that people have the power to change lives. When they realize they have this power, they can begin to help those who are struggling. One of the biggest powers we have is to offer assistance to these individuals. At first, it may feel that this student does not want help, and it may feel like a sense of betrayal. In the end, that friend will appreciate the gesture, and we can rest easily knowing they are receiving the needed help.

When discussing fragile subjects like this, there will always be people on both sides of the fence. The discussion led to some passionate and heated conversations with the class. Some of our classmates felt that when people commit suicide, they are not taking the love and feelings of people around them into account. When people commit suicide, they leave others to mourn. Other students believed these individuals see suicide as the only way out.

I really believe this project helped some to share deep weight baring secrets. On the fourth day of the project, I had a student hand her confession to me personally rather than put it in the box. The question was, "What is something that is misunderstood about you?" This student wrote that she was not happy and that she often thought about ending her life. This situation shows how delicate suicide is. Students do such a great job of hiding their true emotions.

The Sociology students learned a great lesson during this process about the unknown of the people surrounding them. Understanding the experiences and baggage of others around us can help us to become more empathetic. Our knowledge can help us to recognize that we don't know the depth of issues in others, but getting to know them can make all the difference.

I was happy this student was given the opportunity to share this confession. I hope the release of such a big secret gave relief and courage to seek any necessary assistance they may need.

Write a song for someone I love

I heard a great piece of advice from V.J. Smith at an event in Waverly. He told me that most people strive to leave a legacy behind when they pass away. Some want to leave a legacy in history, others on their community, and most with their family and friends. One of the most permanent ways to leave our legacy is to write a book or a song. They are personal expressions that can be revisited and can survive generations. Songs or a book help to sustain one's beliefs, thoughts, and feelings.

For a middle school or high school student to write this confession is something special. Love comes in many different forms. We try to express our feelings to those who are close to us in many ways. Some are very open and honest about their love; some keep to themselves and let their actions speak for them; others are full of affection but struggle to express themselves. But how do we best express our love?

According to Gary Chapman, author of *The Five Love Languages*,[3] five different ways exist to show love to someone: words of affirmation, acts of service, receiving gifts, quality time, and physical touch. I think "writing a song for someone I love" exemplifies this book, especially the words of affirmation and acts of service sections. We need to find our

---

[3] Chapman, Gary D. *The 5 Love Languages*. Northfield Pub., 2015.

strengths and show our feelings through those strengths. For those who are musically inclined, this would be a powerful way to show them affection.

We are always looking for love, both to be given and received, but the first step is to understand the way we express ourselves and how that differs from person to person. When people can understand how they love and how the others around them love, making connections and building relationships becomes less complex. When couples are able to do this, we see them grow and develop a spark. That spark cannot be faked or purchased, it is something that is real and special for those who are able to obtain it.

As we get older and grow together, our love changes for one another. Careers, children, and life in general both strengthen and strain our relationships. Throughout these life changes, I have found that little tokens of appreciation mean even more. Our significant others know we are busy and have many thoughts on our mind, but a simple affirmation reverses the monotony of everyday interactions.

When I think of high school and love songs, I think about couples making mixed tapes or CDs with their favorite love songs on it for their boyfriend or girlfriend. People would listen to these tapes for three weeks straight until the songs made their ears bleed. High school students think promise rings are the way to go to show love for their dating mate, but a mixtape that professes love will win hearts. I remember my older sister got one of these awesome tapes when she was in high school, and it became the soundtrack of our house for at least a month. I remember shooting baskets outside and singing, "And I Will Always Love You" by Whitney Houston. If that song doesn't drive a person to be the best basketball player one can be, I don't know what will.

Not be in constant fear to fail

Everyone reading this book can relate to this confession. Fear is all around us. At times, fear can define who we are. Students and adults alike face fear of failure, fear of embarrassment, fear of change, and fear of rejection in everyday situations.

I have learned so much through this project about students and their similarities with adults. But within the similarities are wide differences. Here is a hypothetical example: there is a twelve-year-old female student and a seventy-five-year-old male who both fear to fail. The student has a deep fear of failing in school and in her activities. When adversity surfaces, this student worries about what her parents, peers, and teachers will think about her. She may struggle to come to school because of the pressure to please everyone. The elderly gentleman has been in retirement now for ten years but struggles to get out of bed because of fear of failure to keep up with the times. He has been known for his intelligence, and at his old age, he is not nearly as sharp. The man fears he will fail, and it will reflect on his legacy, on him, and on his family. He feels if he slips up, he will end up in a nursing home and will lose the freedom he has enjoyed throughout his life. Both of these individuals fear to fail but in very different capacities.

Many instances in our life exist when we have been afraid. Now imagine having that feeling frequently throughout the day. The stress that comes along with failure is overbearing. I try to evaluate this situation from a student's viewpoint. A seventeen-year-old boy gets up in the morning and gets ready for school. The first thing he thinks about is the test he took yesterday and failed. He has a test fourth period and it is worth 15 percent of his entire semester grade. Prom season is coming, and he still has not asked the girl he likes because he is afraid of rejection. He gets to school and finds out that the girl he wanted to ask is going with one of his buddies, and the coach came and told him that he was not going to start because the team wanted to go a different route. These are the stories that are left unsaid and are kept hidden throughout the day. We ask so much of these students when some already have overflowing plates.

Teachers wonder why students are not attentive in class and are frustrated with them about lack of effort. Students, like adults, deal with things every day that bring various stresses into their lives. Adolescents and adults differ in the skills they have developed to deal with stress. Most adolescents do not have the proper coping mechanisms to deal with some of the issues that arise. This can lead to spikes in depression, suicidal ideation, eating disorders, and other mental health issues we see in schools today.

When I first read this confession, I reminisced on my time coaching basketball. I often think student-athletes would perform better if we banned parents from coming to the games. Student athletes tend to struggle when they are not successful, but a major factor some experience is falling short on expectations set at home or in the community. One bad play, quarter, or game can lead to hours of ridicule and disappointment when they get home. This can be hard on students who lack the coping skills that we develop later in life.

Fear can inhibit people from taking the chances necessary to achieve their fullest capabilities. People who become successful take calculated risks to achieve their desired position in life. One goal in education is to give students the opportunity to take chances in a safe environment. We promote students taking risks to be able to achieve their goals in hope that one day, they will be able to do the same in the real world. The material in education covered every day in the classroom is important, but it is the lessons on life and building the social skills necessary to succeed after high school that are perhaps the most important.

What makes a meaningful life?

After reading the various confessions, I have come to the conclusion that adolescents and adults strive to achieve common goals in life, those goals are just in different contexts. Imagine what sort of answers students in a middle school and high school would answer when asked this question. Impressed with some of the answers I read, I related to a majority of them. We don't give students as much credit as they deserve. Most are driven and know what they want in life. This prompt allows us to see the purpose and drive of students.

The second prompt had sixty-five responses. Some of those responses include the following: living life to the fullest, having people to love, supporting people, having courage to get through things, feeling accomplished in life, enjoying summer, eating nachos, trusting relationships, and being satisfied with who we are. Each answer had a story behind it and helped to make their lives meaningful.

This project and how the students responded brought meaning to my life. At the end of the day, I wanted to look back and know that I impacted lives and that I helped people along the way. That is why educators get into the profession. We love when students come back and thank us for the time, energy, and love we put into them and that we made a difference.

We all strive to make our lives meaningful, but each of us see meaningful in a different light. We spend our time trying to find what is important to us and embrace it as much as possible. Those who are able to keep focus on their priorities, such as family, friends, and faith, are those who will likely find happiness.

After reading some of these confessions, I felt a sense of relief come over me knowing that our students, with these sort of values and ideals, will go on to live meaningful lives. When students have direction, it makes their journey to achieve their goals much easier. I thought that these seven confessions showed how great students are and how well they compare to adults.

Finding the positivity in things

"Today, have you focused on the positives in your life more than the negatives?" That was the question that arose when this confession was read to the class. It is easier said than done to stay positive through various experiences throughout our life. When we think negatively, it gives us an excuse if we happen to fail. Finding the positives can be just as easy as finding the negatives in events if we train ourselves to do so. When we do face adversity, it can be habit to make excuses for shortcomings. People can be there to help support, but in the end it is our responsibility to come out of situations and grow from the experience. When we can grow, we will begin to locate the positives in life much more frequently. Occurrences come up where the negatives outweigh the positives; that is why it is so important to embrace the good aspects of our lives and celebrate them when they do come along.

Finding the positivity in things is a habit that can be developed over time. In my first years of teaching, I began to live by a saying I picked up from a gentleman I met. He said to me, "If that is the worst thing that happens today, we are going to have a pretty good day." That saying is spot on. The phrase has helped me to put occurrences into perspective and has allowed me to let the little incidences slide. We let the little things get under our skin, and when positive opportunities come our way, we tend to be blinded by the negativity in our lives. Being proactive proves crucial to being a positive person.

When we go out and look for the good in life, it is unbelievable how much we tend to find.

We all know people who find the good in everything. They are positive people who enjoy the simple things in life. When I think about people who enjoy the little things, I think about children opening their presents on Christmas. People will spend large amounts of money to get their children what they want, and what do these kids play with? Cardboard boxes. To adults, cardboard boxes are bound for the trash. The only time we see the positives in these boxes are when we are packing up our belongings to move. But through the eyes of children, these boxes are immaculate. Positives in our world are noticed at a higher rate by children than adults. These boxes can be a race car winning the Daytona 500, they can be a mansion they just built after winning the lottery, they can be a spaceship just about to land on the moon, or they could be a tree fort that dad had promised to build, but just can't find the time.

I understand people need to have a realistic view of themselves and the situations around them, but why can't we open our mind to opportunity and positivity like children can? Children see the good in everything. They take risks and chances on the opportunities in front of them because they think the world is safe. They put trust in their parents and the people around them to protect them during tough times. As we get older, we lose faith in situations and the people with whom we surround ourselves. We begin to lose the sense of invincibility and become vulnerable. The negativity surrounding us in everyday life becomes more prevalent, and we begin to dwell on it. Those who are able to open their minds without the fear of negativity will lessen their stress and they will tend to find a great deal of happiness.

Leaving a legacy

All people strive to leave some sort of legacy behind when they pass. Legacy is comprehended differently among many different groups of people. When I asked the class what their definition of legacy was, I received mixed feedback. Some stated a legacy had to do with assets left behind. Others believed a legacy is what we are remembered by when we pass away. In the dictionary, legacy is defined as the money or property left to someone in a will. After reading this definition, we as a class agreed there was much more to this definition than was listed in the dictionary.

When looking at life and what we leave behind, people begin to think about that for which they wish to be remembered. As adults, our career tends to align with our legacy. The good work we have done for a company or an organization tends to go with us until we die. But how long will that legacy last after we have passed? People who leave a lasting legacy are those who have made changes or conducted an act that has impacted the people of their time and for future generations. When characteristics of these people are discussed, the same ones keep appearing. These people tend to have passion for what they are doing, they care about the people around them, and they are very supportive.

We began talking about the people who have graced our lives and the legacy they have left behind. The first person I think about was a friend of mine who passed away due to cancer. I always thought a long life was crucial when leaving a solid legacy; however, this man proved me wrong. On April 30, a celebration of his life and the beginning of his legacy was held in a full house at the Barnett Center in Aberdeen. His impact in the community and school led to his baseball number being retired at Fossum Field in Aberdeen and a golf tournament held on his behalf each year. The way he lived his life with no fear and enjoyed every minute he lived moved me. What is even more impressive is the way he built relationships that still have lasting impacts. People who only spoke with him on a few occasions were impacted by the news of his passing. He never took anyone or anything for granted; that is what made him special.

He passed in April 2012, and people continue to post on his Facebook page about memories they had with him. These people come across things in their daily lives that remind them of him five years later; that is powerful. A man who was taken from us too soon still had the time to touch our lives and push us to become better people. Although my journey has taken me down a different path, I know he is one with whom I would have continued to build a relationship. He had the ability to impact people's day by just saying hi. I knew this man for a little over two years, but he changed me for the better. I consider him one of my top five most influential people who has graced my life. When influential people present themselves, embrace them. Take the time to get to know them and enjoy their company. Those people's presence and influence is not always a guarantee.

When people to whom we are close to and respect pass away, their legacy becomes desirable by those of us left behind. Subconsciously, I went into education because my grandpa was a teacher and superintendent in the town in which I grew up. He was always teaching me something new and interesting. He taught me concepts about carpentry, history, leisure activities, and so much more. His legacy consisted of being an educator and the information he instilled on everyone who met him. He was one of the most caring people I have ever met and wanted to help solve problems. He received a sense of accomplishment when he would help someone struggling. Many people came up to him years after he had retired and thanked him for caring and being present in their lives. He found what he set out to find in life and embraced the journey.

At times, the journey and the accomplishments along the way can be more satisfying than the final goal. As an educator, our legacy is left behind with the students we touch and the relationships we build. Each student's success is a process, with bumps along the way. Our interactions and relationships differ among students; therefore, our legacy will vary with those students.

How is a legacy determined? People can look at what they focus their time on and their priorities when trying to determine what their legacy will be when they pass. When people spend a great time at work and put their time and effort into that, it will become part of their legacy they will leave behind. When people focus on their children and support them, they become part of their legacy. We need to ask ourselves an important question:

Does the way I spend my time match my values and priorities? If it does, I believe we will be satisfied with the image and legacy we leave behind.

Student Comment
All seniors desire to leave a legacy. Leaving a legacy on my school when I am completed would be a step in achieving a meaningful life.

Having someone with whom to share it

Success is nothing without having someone to share it with; I can attest to this. In my short life, I have always had someone with whom to share my successes. I was fortunate enough to have two parents and two siblings in my house who cared about me and my accomplishments. They were there to celebrate the success and console in the failures. They taught me how to accept defeat and enjoy the successes. The first thing I wanted to do after achieving a goal in high school was share it with my family. I appreciated the support I received from those who were close to me.

This changed when I began dating my wife Shari in high school. I began to reach out to her for assistance when problems arose. She complements me. She has been there for me through thick and thin and is true to herself. She is caring to the people around her and cares about their wellbeing. I know when I bring good news home, she will help to celebrate and truly feels happy for me. I know when misfortune hits, she will be the first to help me persevere. Home should be welcoming and promote security, and I could not ask more from Shari.

We develop many skills at an early age before we start school; one of those skills we develop is building and maintaining relationships. The status of our relationships both present and past mold how we go out and build relationships moving forward. Early in my life, I took for granted the relationships that benefited me. I took for granted what those relationships provided me growing up. Now I see students struggle to obtain strong relationships, and it helps me to appreciate the ones I have. I try to make connections with struggling students to help them along the way. One of the most important skills we as educators can teach students is how to build solid relationships and how to maintain them throughout their life.

Being part of healthy relationships is important. They help to promote success, while unhealthy relationships can be our demise as we move forward. Initially when I read this confession, I thought about Shari first. It made me think about all the relationships I have formed over the years and the ones that have helped me along the way. I also thought about the relationships from which I have disconnected. It is proven that people are what they associate with. The people one spends time with will begin to reflect on one's personality. I have chosen to spend time with people who play a positive role in my life. Negativity is something that wears on people. If Shari was not as positive as she is, I don't believe being completely open and honest with her would be as easy.

Another thought that crossed my mind was the elderly couple who splits a hamburger at the local Perkins and sits on the same side of the booth. They wouldn't say a word to each other the entire time, they just really enjoyed each other's company. Those two individuals know everything about one another. I have also learned how our affection and dependency changes for one another as we get older. I think about their journey and the ups and downs they endured along the way.

"In today's society, making it to this booth is something to speak for."

Students need to have people with whom to share their successes and misfortunes, whether it be parents, friends, siblings, or someone they trust. Are they in a place to share their achievements and receive comfort during times of stress? Students, as well as adults, need a place to release their thoughts, needs, and aspirations in a caring environment. When they have that person or people with whom to share those thoughts, they are more likely to step out of the box and try new experiences. When we are in this situation, we tend to observe some of the biggest surprises in our life.

I asked the students in the sociology class if they had these people at this moment. Some of the students said their parents served that role, others said siblings, one said friends, and one student in class said she used to. The class discussion then shifted to how the people we share everything with change throughout our lives. We grow up, move away from home, meet new people, fall in love, fall out of love, and throughout those transitions, the people on whom we rely changes. They become more aligned with our personalities, values, and goals.

How do we know when we "have someone with whom to share it?" When something happens in our lives, we are more excited about sharing the information with that someone than actually receiving the news. We think about how the person will respond. When the people we spend our time with begin to be people we share "it" with, our hearts fill with love. We feel at ease when we know that person is in our corner.

Being able to answer why

I have always been one of those guys who needs to be told "why" before I will completely buy-in. When we understand the "why," we begin to take ownership in the concept. "Why" is a question we learn at an early age. We hear our children ask why about 300 times a day from ages 2-3. These children find out the importance of this question and want to know how the world works. We as adults can relate to this. We feel if we are able to answer this question why, we will understand our purpose in the process. When we are able to understand our purpose in life, our goals become much clearer, and our journey to achieve those goals becomes that much easier.

We encounter various experiences that require us to take a step back and examine why. The step back will give us insight into the situation and reinforce or deter our behavior moving forward. People in all different walks of life will answer the question differently. The experiences we encounter throughout life and our belief system we have established will help to identify the why in things.

I am a member of a local Catholic Church where we attend regularly. My beliefs within our church have changed my perspective on different ideas and helped me to answer why. I believe religion and/or beliefs play a large role in a person's success. People do not need to be religious to be successful, but they need something in which to believe; they need to have hope in something. Religion offers me a sense of hope; hope that in the end everything will be all right. It gives me purpose on why things happen the way they do. I believe everything happens for a reason, and when we experience misfortune, our faith is being tested and strengthened. Many verses in the Bible explain the importance of challenges we face and how failing can ultimately make us stronger in the end.

In some instances, we search endlessly, but cannot seem to find the answers to some of these questions. There may not be a clear answer, but the lessons we learn along the way can be magnifying. The experiences we come across and the obstacles we encounter while searching for these answers are what define us. I know a family who has shown me the importance of the journey and how that makes us who we are. This family has two children. One child, a middle-school boy who has shown through the years how big his heart is. The other child, a sweet fourth-grade girl who has a heart of gold. Who would have known when the little girl was born that she would change the lives of people around her? For years, she was diagnosed with ADHD and OHI (other health impairments), which led to a lack of support for her. Last year, she was identified on the autistic spectrum.

Many times through their life, the family probably wondered, "why us"? I have been with this family for five years and have seen the ups and downs they have experienced. But why? Why her? Why her family; here is why. She was put on this earth to help people, in which she has. She is here to show us how to love with our whole heart. She has taught me a lot about passion for the things I enjoy. She has opened my eyes to perspective and priorities. She has changed my life, and I appreciate the time I have spent with her. As she grows, she will continue to teach me lessons of life and how to live mine. The sad part is she will never truly understand the impact she has had on my life and those around her.

We are in constant search for the answer to why. We look at every alternative as to why something happen. Sometimes answers will not be found. This goes against the concept we learn at a very young age to understand the reason why. We rely on our faith and understanding of people, but there are times where no explanations will be found. At this point, it is crucial to be able to accept the fact and move forward. People who let this feeling linger tend to struggle, and it creates complications in their daily living.

Our class then took a completely different view on this confession. We discussed concepts with no answer as to why it happened.

At times, believing things will get better may be the only light that we have.

I asked the class if they thought it was all right to not have the answer as to why things are the way they are. Some of the students shared they felt some questions were better left unanswered. They liked the realm of the unknown, and it pushed them to draw their own conclusions.

Being able to climb the mountains that life has to offer

We all have come across issues that seem somewhat insurmountable. Adversity hits, and we are left to figure out the next steps. We must rely on the people we trust and care for to help us on our climb. I have been blessed with a solid support group throughout my life. As a kid, I had a community that looked out for me; my success was their success. As I went off to college, I had friends whom I could trust and had the opportunity to build great relationships with them. As I moved on and got married and had children, I was supported by close friends and my family. Mountains seem much smaller when climbing with people who are caring and supportive.

Where do we receive the motivation and push to help with the climb? Some receive their drive by trying to prove people wrong. Others are pushed to climb by those around them. I have been lucky enough to have someone to share that climb with me. She not only climbs with me but also pushes me to climb higher than I ever thought I could. The success I achieve throughout life can be a reflection of the support I receive from people close to me, especially my wife.

I have always been a guy who looks at the glass "half-full" as opposed to "half-empty." This confession shows us that our mindset and how we perceive instances will show us how we will solve problems going forward.

The mindset of the climber plays a role in how big their mountain is.

When one makes the mountain seem achievable, it becomes much more feasible. On the other hand, many people can make the hills in their lives into mountains. A mindset is something that can be altered through various events we experience. One of the biggest factors in building our mindset is those with whom we spend our time. When we spend time with positive people, we tend to see the light in things. Their positive views on life rub off on us, and we begin taking on some of their characteristics. When we spend time with those who make mountains out of molehills, we tend to grasp that mindset, and that influences our lives in a negative way.

The climb consists of the challenges and adversity one will face along the way. Going down the hill is a celebration of the perseverance and endurance shown during the climb. When people tend to embrace the downhill slope more than the climb, they find themselves not climbing as often. The climb can be directly correlated to the negativity we face in life.

When people dwell on the climb, they tend to lose sight in what they are climbing for.

While reading this confession, I look at what this student has had to overcome in his or her life. The students in our sociology class have had to overcome some mountains throughout their lives. Because of prior experiences among the class, this confession initiated deep conversation and discussion. This is when the students in the class began to look at some of the experiences of their peers. We talked about how those experiences can play a role in the development of their personality. If students would look at some of the circumstances students are faced with on a daily basis, they may hesitate to judge some of the students; they may even begin to respect them. When we become aware of the situations around us, our mountains in our lives begin to shrink. It also helps those individuals to feel like they are not alone.

This confession encouraged me to recall some of the people I have had a privilege to know and some of the mountains these people have had to climb. I look at one of the buddies I lost along the way and his parents; his parents went through hell. No parent should have to experience burying their 22-year-old child. At the time, I knew these two were suffering, but did not understand until having a child of my own on how difficult the tragedy would have been for those two parents. I don't know how these two were able to climb this mountain, but the faith they had in each other, in God, and in their son's life and legacy is inspirational. They use his journey and the people who cared for him to help them along the healing process. As I check on his Caring Bridge site frequently, I see sparing posts from his dad. His last post read:

High fives - good

5 years missing....

April 24 2012 - April 24 2017

Not so good.........

This is a climb that will continue throughout their lives. I pray these parents find the strength to endure the daily battle they face each day.

Finding my faith

Faith is a dynamic and powerful word. The definition of faith is to have complete trust or confidence in someone or something. So why does finding faith lead to a meaningful life? In the end, we all look back on how we spent our time, what we accomplished, and what we achieved. We also look at what we believed in and in what we instilled our faith. A meaningful life consists of looking back on our prior beliefs and seeing merit. When we see that the concepts we grew up instilling our faith in were true, we start to see meaning in our life. It gives us self-satisfaction.

When a couple gets married, they put faith in one another, through sickness and in health. Many marriages also use the faith of God in their marriage as strength to endure anything they come across. When we climb the mountains that life has to offer, we use our faith in one another to overcome. As we know, faith strengthens or declines through the years. But why? Why does the faith we put in someone decline over the years? Why do fifty percent of marriages end in divorce? Faith plays a large role in the success of marriage, and without faith, marriages will struggle to survive.

When things are hard in our life, faith may be the only thing we have to keep us pushing forward

What type of faith is this student trying to find? Is this student trying to find faith in a divine source? Is this student trying to find faith in people? Or just all of the above? So many students try to find faith in various sources. They have been betrayed in the past by people and beliefs in their life and struggle to trust going forward. When we do not have trusting relationships, we struggle to build skills that will help us succeed. For example, toddlers take chances as they develop because they have faith in their surroundings and have confidence that someone will be there to help them. As adults, we need that same support. We need faith in our surroundings and the people around us to develop. We need faith to take risks and chances to advance ourselves as individuals.

I look back on my journey while finding my faith. I was one who did not go to church regularly on Sundays. I did go every Wednesday to evening church classes, and that helped to build a foundation of where I am today. Just like any kid, I went because I had to. I understood the purpose of church but didn't get a ton out of it. As I grew older, the overall teachings of the church became much clearer, and I realized why I wanted to attend. The church and its teachings gave me a sense of hope and faith in things after life. It gave me an explanation of why the world is how it is. Church offered me a solid set of values to establish in my life and instill in my family's life.

The beautiful aspect of the church is those attending church actually want to be there. With this comes the lift of negativity. Sure there are disputes going on in churches, but for the most part, a church symbolizes peace and positivity. Think about places we visit on a weekly basis. It will be extremely hard to find a place that provides this sort of environment; an environment filled with hope and faith. I understand religion and the church setting is not for everyone, but in this world, we need a place outside of the home where people can come together in a positive light and share their faith. Finding this place will help lead to a happy life.

I asked the class for their definition of faith. Although the answers were somewhat similar from each of the students, small differences changed the whole concept of faith. Everyone has a different idea of what faith is and what it means in their life. We then began talking about the people and figures in which they put their faith. Many said God, friends, family, and hope. They again had mostly the same answers, but in different orders and priorities. I later asked the students about a time they lost faith in something; the room went silent.

Admitting we have lost faith is hard. It shows us we are vulnerable; it shows people we have been hurt.

One of the students mentioned they had lost faith in lasting love. They have been around many relationships which ended in divorce and heartbreak. I hope for the sake of this student that he or she can find people to put faith back into love, because a strong love in those around us leads to a successful and happy life.

As teens, we don't start to understand or appreciate our faith until it is tested. The same can be said for adults as well. In those situations, we either strengthen our faith or begin to lose it. Many instances we come across test our faith. Disagreements, sickness, accidents, and dishonesty are all examples of adversity that will test our faith in people, places, things, or ideas. A solid support system and a strong foundation of faith will help us through these various situations.

Having no regrets at the end

The definition of regret changes for people depending on their background. Some believe regrets originated from the situations in which we are placed. Others believe regrets stem from the wrong decisions we have made throughout our lives. They think if they would have made different decisions, their life would have changed for the better. Human nature causes us to second guess ourselves. When we put so much importance on each decision we make, we tend to lose sight of what we want to accomplish in our lives.

I like to look at regrets as deeds left undone. This allows me to focus on efforts I can still accomplish, rather than dwelling on decisions I have made in the past.

When we allow negative aspects of our past to impact us, these features can impact our future. An example of this would be losing someone we love. I lost a friend of mine to cancer. The first response was regretting how we lost touch and thought about some of the things that were left unsaid. It was tough, but I needed to understand there was nothing I could change about the memories or experiences we made, but there was still an opportunity for personal growth. My priority was to not feel like this again; a void that was left after this friend had passed. I needed to stay in touch with people who were close to me and continue to build new relationships as well. When we are able to do this, our relationships will become stronger and the experiences we encounter will be more notable. Each time I catch up with a friend with whom I have lost touch, the friend I lost years prior still comes to mind.

I stopped at a gas station outside Sioux Falls, South Dakota, on my way home from a college class on a Saturday afternoon. I had to stop and grab a beverage for the road. As soon as I walked in, I noticed an attendant who was helping a different customer. The questions she asked and the way she spoke with him was moving; I wanted to go through her line. I was the third person in her line and listened closely to her encounters with each guest. In that short time, I understood one thing, this woman was special. She may have had regrets in life, but she went out each day trying to prove something, and she did. If all employees put their heart and soul into what they did and knew they were making a difference, they would have no regrets at the end. She let those who went through her line feel cared for and appreciated. For that, I hope she can look back on life with no regrets and appreciate the work she has done.

In class, I asked the students about regrets in their lives. I wanted the students to look at their regrets and see how it has impacted them. Are they regrets they will think about ten years from now? Are they regrets that challenge their values? Are they regrets that hurt loved ones? If the regret is not worthy, it is not something on which we should dwell. If they felt as though it was something that would define them in the future, I challenged them come up with a plan to make amends to the situation.

I have only been in the education field for a few years, but I have come to the realization that making decisions is a constant occurrence. Some of the decisions I have made could be looked back on and I could wonder if I had made the right decision. We need to be able to make decisions and move forward with our ultimate goal in mind. It is important to accept where we are in our profession and be proud of the accomplishments we have achieved, but to not settle. We need to continue to improve and grow as people.

When we look back on life and have regrets, it often leads to us looking at who we are. The decisions we make define us. When we start questioning the decisions we have made in the past, and later have regrets about those decisions, we begin to question our identity. Students want to be able to look back and be proud of what they have accomplished; every person deserves that right. All people who ponder their past deserve the opportunity to feel as though they left an impact. They deserve the chance to feel like they helped someone; they left a legacy. They need to feel as though their time is well spent, and they can appreciate what they have accomplished. If death were to call me today, I can say that there would be no better feeling than to have my accomplishments and pride trump the regrets in my life.

Student Comment

Acting in this way seems very intelligent. When we live a life of constant worry, we don't seem to find as much happiness.

On what one thing in life have you given up?

Students in schools across the country come from many different backgrounds. The experiences they have come across and some of the relationships they have built have led them to give up on aspects of their life. Some of the confessions submitted dealt with occurrences at school, others dealt with issues at home, and others had much to do with their self-esteem and self-image. Some of the confessions included the following: finding someone who won't do wrong to me, my family, school, my sister, losing weight, basketball, politics, being a country star, bringing people back from the dead, narcissistic people, and trying to be skinny.

This was the third day of our sociology project, but it was the first day our prompt had a negative connotation. Most people have no problem sharing good aspects of their life, but when we begin discussing the negative, people tend to hesitate. The lunch room was a little quieter than normal, which meant students were strongly considering things in their life on which they had given up.

I enjoyed this project because it gave students a place to share their thoughts. For some of these students, this ten minutes proved to be the only time they could be true to themselves and share what they thought; it was therapeutic. They liked the chance for someone to read it and let their problem be known, but appreciated that no one knew it was them. It forced students to take a step back and really look at themselves in the mirror. I am sure it got students thinking about what they have given up on and how that impacted them.

The students were to turn in their confessions in the cardboard box at the end of lunch. On this day, I had a student come to me and hand me a confession between classes in the hallway. I was taken back by this. I did not want to read the confession in the hall, so I waited for the students to report to class and went into my office. This confession stated,

"People, my life and my purpose, I often think what it would be like if I were not here"

It scared me at first, but then I realized this is what this student needed. She needed someone to tell and was searching for guidance. I reported it to the counselor and was thanked a few days later by the student who handed me the confession. When she thanked me, I was puzzled. I commended her on her strength in asking for help. She understood that she was in a dark place and used this project as a way to step out of her comfort zone and reach out. Students like these are the ones who go on and find success. They have experienced various states of mind and will be able to connect to a wider population.

I thought this mix of seven confessions showed how all students differ and how their upbringing and situations play a role in their thoughts and dreams. One thing that surprised me through the project was the wide variety of answers we received. Could one imagine the variety we would receive if we polled a larger population?

My dad

He is the one who takes us fishing for the first time. He is the one who chases boys away from his daughter. He tends to be the calmest person in the room during times of crisis. He is one to whom we look when we have problems. When he is around, nothing can go wrong. His name is dad. Everyone deserves a father figure like this, someone they can look to when they need advice and guidance. They deserve to remember their dad as one of the best men they have ever met. Unfortunately, this isn't the case for some people around the world.

As children, we naturally think our parents are the best people; they can do no wrong. We have all heard country songs of little boys looking up to their dads and doing everything they do because, one day, they want to be just like them. When these individuals in our life are positive role models, the values we learn are much stronger, and the relationships we build have stronger foundations. When those individuals act as bad influences or lead us down the wrong path, it sets the stage for our development into adulthood. Our parents are key examples of how to live our life. We see how they behave and how they parent, and it impacts us in the present time and into the future as well.

Daughters will look for a partner who has similar attributes of their father. When we love someone, we need to be comfortable and secure. Many women loved their fathers greatly; they look for the same attributes to provide themselves a sense of safety and security. Sons will model themselves after their father, for better or worse. They seek approval in all their activities from their father, and this will promote good behavior if used properly.

We can only be burned so many times, but we tend to give those close to us more chances. The reason we struggle to give up on these people is that they have built our identity, and they have impacted us so much. When we give up on them, we feel as though we are losing a part of ourselves in the process. This is why we see people stay in hurtful relationships; they feel as though giving up is the last step and it would lead to failing. When we give up on someone we love, like our father, we are coming to realization we can't overcome a certain situation, which is hard to do. We also tend to remember the positive aspects of the people we love, which can inhibit us from making healthy decisions for ourselves. I am curious what issue this father had; why did this student give up on his or her dad? What did he do to destroy the numerous bridges built by his daughter or son? What sort of lasting impact did this dad leave on this student and how will that play a role in his or her development moving forward.

In education, these students come from many backgrounds: one or two-parent households, supportive households, households not engaged in the student's life, foster care, abusive families, and everything in between. Either way, a father or lack thereof plays a role in all these situations. A relationship with a father can make or break the entire education, and ultimately the life, of a student.

The troubling part of parenting is the fathers who know the importance of being present, still they struggle to deliver. They see their children struggle academically, mentally, and emotionally but yet don't make changes that will benefit their children. This may go back to how they were parented growing up. They may have not received adequate care and support, and are just mirroring their childhood.

I have a buddy who had given up on his real father at an early age. This story explains how important a father figure is in the development of children. While he was growing up, my buddy had a dad who battled alcoholism. During a time in his life when he was to look up to his dad, he was not there. Many times throughout his life he was promised support and guidance, and his father was nowhere to be found. The older brothers served as father figures and did a great job. The mother raised four boys well all by herself and did what she could, until another man came along. He was one of the most dependable and caring men whom I have had the honor to know. He took them as his own and served as a strong role model for them. The boys responded well and respected him. If a person asked him, he would say he wanted it no other way. It would be interesting to see where this family was if this man would not have come along. With how strong the mother is and the great personalities the boys have, they would have grown up just fine, but without a supporting father figure, the boys would have missed out on important life lessons and would not have been able to build memories that last a lifetime.

Strong father figures offer their children so much. They comfort them when they are down, they guide them to be the best person they can be, they teach them lessons and skills that they will use the rest of their lives, and they will protect them along the way. With this sort of figure present, learning and developing becomes much easier for children throughout the world. We need to take this sort of circumstance into consideration when dealing with people. Some people we come across were not lucky enough to have this sort of figure in their life and are still trying to find that person in their life.

Making everyone happy

Human nature calls us to please people. We receive satisfaction when people are impressed with our efforts and our actions. In school, this becomes even more magnified. Students are constantly trying to impress their peers. To do that, the people around them have to be impressed with something they offer. This can lead to us building a false identity. I see this a great deal in school. Students are willing to sacrifice everything to make people around them happy. Life is easier in school when people are accepting. We just hope these students are able to stay true to themselves during this process.

I often think about what students are willing to do to make people happy. What did this student do? How many sleepless nights came along this student's journey of acceptance, thinking about changes they can make to fit in? Every student who comes through the doors has a different story and different experiences. Some students try extremely hard to be accepted into their class. Why is it so important for students to fit in? At that age, students are trying to find their purpose and identity. If they can receive acceptance along their journey, it will make it much easier to take chances.

The hardest lesson to teach students is that they have the power to make people's day. These students make decisions every day that can impact the people around them. They have the opportunity to impact learning, boost confidence, change perceptions, influence, and even save lives. When students use this power in a positive light, school is an enjoyable place to be. The students and staff are happy, the school begins to improve academically, and the extracurricular programs thrive. Not only do students have this power, but also adults do. We have the power to change the days of those around us. Those who are able to embrace this truly make a difference.

One of the greatest feelings, yet one of the hardest feelings to accomplish, is being able to make people happy while staying true to oneself. Throughout the journey, we are forced to make decisions based on what we believe is right. With some of those decisions will come displeasure. We encounter many experiences throughout our day and we have to make a decision on how we are going to let it impact us.

All teachers have students whom they can identify as a "people pleasers." I had a student who would do anything to make the people around him happy. He was a kid who had a tough home life but came to school with his game face on and worked hard to build relationships with the students around him. I respect his efforts despite the ridicule he encounters each day. These students who give him grief don't understand the damage they do. Each day he comes to school, he loses faith in people. He begins to think regardless of what he does, he will not be able to make people happy. We are in a world where not all people can be trusted and good deeds often go unnoticed. I am afraid this student will learn this and change. All it takes is one person to step up and thank him for being him and not to change. That one person can be anyone willing to step up and help someone. This person can be developed in an instant and can change the days of numerous people.

As we grow older, we begin to understand the pursuit of making everyone happy is unreachable. No matter what we do, someone will be unpleased with our efforts, our abilities, or the outcome. I learned from one of my mentors, John Bjorkman, that if we try to please everyone, we will please no one. We must do what we believe and let the people around us help us achieve. Those who are able to consider the efforts and thought process behind a decision, and at the end respect it, are those we want close to us.

Forgiving him

We want to put our trust in those with whom we spend our time. We rely on those people to help us through tough times and be there for us when we need support. When these people do not deliver on their expectations, we may get upset with them, and trust can be broken. This leads to the gift of forgiveness. Forgiveness is a skill we develop over time and can use on a daily basis.

The experiences we encounter, the relationships that we have built, and our personality all play a role in how we forgive people and how long it will take to forgive them.

Our life stories are all different. We have all had to forgive people in some capacity. Forgiveness needs to be cherished because it can lose its power when we have to use it too much. Many people we come across struggle to forgive. They have opened up their heart to people by forgiving them and have been hurt too many times. This can lead to trust issues, and those people will struggle to build strong relationships because of their past experiences. This student has continued to forgive "him" and has now given up on this.

The act of forgiveness changes throughout our life. As a child, forgiving is instinct. We forgive because we can't fathom being upset with people for a long period of time. We rely on these people so much that there is no other option other than to forgive. As we get older, we put our trust in people and sometimes are disappointed. The more we are disappointed, the harder it is to trust and forgive. I have found that as adults, our levels of trust and forgiveness are based on past experiences. We are careful with whom we let in our life and even more careful on whom we let back into our life when they have done us wrong.

I have never understood how some people are able to forgive the ones they love for their actions in the past. Spouses who encounter abuse will continue to go back to their husbands or wives despite the constant belittling and making them feel unworthy. I have had the opportunity to work with a special individual who fits this story well. She is one of the strongest people I know, and I admire her. She was in one of these relationships. Her state of mind throughout this relationship was of defeat; she felt trapped. She continued to forgive him because she wanted the relationship to go back to how they used to be; she wanted to see the light and make things right. She felt if she gave up on him, she was giving up on herself as well, so she continued to forgive. She was most afraid that if she did not forgive him, this "mess" would be revealed to the people she loved.

She turned to God during her troubled times. She realized every time she forgave him for his actions, she lost a little courage inside. She was being depleted in all facets of her life, and she felt confined. She used God to help her through the darkness. She surrounded herself with positive people and began to pull herself out. She finally overcame this destructive relationship when she realized the fear of the unknown became less than the fear she was living. I hope one day she can forgive him for the pain and misery he put her through. For her to move on with her life and appreciate things she is able to accomplish, she will have to forgive him.

Throughout this project, I have asked students to put themselves in each of these confessions. We then walked through a day in their life and how our perceptions of people align with their actual life. We have students who go home and struggle to trust people in their families and cannot forgive them. We have people in relationships who struggle to forgive their partner for something hurtful they did. These students come with this sort of experience to school every day and are asked to put their trust in students and teachers to learn. Some students are at such a disadvantage with the baggage they have to carry around with them that learning is on the bottom of their list of priorities. Their ability to leave baggage at the door and achieve at a high level in school is commendable; we tend to not give students enough credit for their courage and strength.

A fine line is drawn between the inability to forgive and the tendency to forgive to easily. Although the struggle to forgive as adults is human nature, it is essential to be able to do it to build strong relationships. When we use our mistakes and learn from them, it can help build the relationships in our life. Part of the success in a relationship is defined by the mistakes made and how the couple was able to overcome them. When a partner in the marriage struggles to forgive their spouse, the relationship tends to be unhealthy. As couples grow older together, the trust they have instilled in each other throughout their lives will help them to forgive and move on.

<u>Student Comment</u>
I can personally relate to this confession. I dated a boy for two years and just recently went through a breakup. It's hard to forgive him almost a year and a half later for what he said and did to me after we broke up.

Being good enough

We are in a society that promotes this confession. Everything we do in life is compared to those around us. We promote competition in all aspects of life. This is a good concept to promote people to be the best they can be, but I have seen the negative effects in education. To prepare students, we tend to implement competition in school. Students are told at an early age they do not do things as well as their peers; this can be detrimental later in life. These students are compared to other students of various intellectual levels and asked to achieve at the same level. For most students, this is impossible. When we base success on this, only a select few have outstanding high school accomplishments; the rest are just along for the ride. In a perfect world, we gauge each student's success and appreciate the individual growth witnessed throughout school, but we are so focused on preparing students for the competition of the real world. This practice does not build students and their confidence to give them esteem to push forward but labels them at an early age. It tells students they are not good enough at an early age and does not give them the chance to prove the system wrong. This system can lay the groundwork moving forward.

Expectations are a fact of life. Our parents set expectations for us to live by, our teachers set expectations to help us succeed in school, our bosses set expectations for us to be efficient and effective, and society sets expectations for us to live by. When the people we are around set high expectations for us, it challenges us to be the best person we can become. We need to meet expectations to build ourselves up and give us the confidence to move forward.

Not meeting our expectations set for us is an obstacle of life, but how we deal with that sets the stage for how we will continue on.

If we allow missed expectations to impact us, it can lead to struggles. As my sister was going through her early twenties, she made a few mistakes. I preached to her the importance of moving forward with a clear mind. She needed to understand the mistake has been made and her character will be revealed in how she deals with the aftermath. I told her to not allow this mistake to lead her down a path that she would not appreciate, and that she is in control of her journey.

I heard a story about a man who had committed suicide. He was in a family of four with great and supportive parents. His three siblings were great athletes, good students, and everything just seemed to line up for them. This man had to work hard for everything he received and caught some misfortune along the way. The expectations set were very high because of what his siblings had done. His efforts were good but not as good as his siblings. He lived in their shadows and there was no way out. He was tired of not being able to live up to the expectations set for him and took his own life.

We have students in this situation all over the nation. We set extremely high expectations for them; some meet them, others do not. The problem with these expectations is they come at a time when life is moving so fast.

They do not have the coping mechanisms to deal with adversity. It is important to challenge students and expect great things out of them, but setting these goals can also be their demise. Everywhere students look, there are expectations they must achieve to be deemed "successful." I have seen some students who struggled to meet those expectations at an early age and that has resulted in very little effort in the classroom and in their daily operations in general. They allow their struggles in school to cross over to other aspects of life.

We see the confessional play out all too often. When people work hard and come up short of the expectations set for them, they lose confidence in themselves. If they feel as though the people around them think they are not good enough, they begin to believe this. "Not being good enough" is a mindset established by past experiences we have encountered. They feel as though their time is not as valuable and will not amount to anything sustainable.

Failure is something we all encounter in our life. When failure is encountered, our true character reveals itself. When we are told we are not good enough, we have two choices: We can allow that to hurt and it can hold us back, or we can allow it to put a chip on our shoulder. The decision we make will play a role in our success. An example would be of influential figures, such as Walt Disney, seeing failure early on in life and not allowing that to define their success. Sometimes we need to fail to keep us motivated.

When people are afraid of failure, they have a tendency to not put in full effort. This will give them an excuse when things did not turn out the way they expected. Excuses can play a large role in failure. When we fail, we look for reasoning and understanding; that is when excuses begin to reveal themselves. Excuses allow us to give understanding on why something happened without putting the blame solely on ourselves; this hides the true solution to the problem. Those who seek and tend to find success are those who look at their failures and ask questions about why and how it happened. They look at their role in the failure and ask themselves what they could do to help it become a success.

Trying to make friends

We all know how important friends are in our lives. A happy and enjoyable life tends to be accompanied with many friends. When we do not have people in our lives, we struggle to receive the support we need. Meeting good friends can dictate our outlook on our jobs, school, and community. The absences of those types of people in our life can also lead to high stress. We don't have anyone to talk to outside our house about issues, advice, or interests. Sometimes with our students, the most positive place in their lives is outside the house, so good friends are crucial for their success and well-being.

Making new friends can be exciting yet stressful. Students tend to have a few months when they first move to a school to make connections and begin fitting in. Think about the pressure on some of these students. They were just pulled away from their roots and friends. Everything in the world that is normal to these students has changed, and some have to search for themselves. We also ask these students to learn the styles of new teachers, new peers, new expectations, and be successful. The building of solid friendships can help with this transition immensely. When these students find their group, academics will likely take care of themselves. But, what if they don't find anyone? The famous statement "It is not what we know, it is who we know" plays strongly into this concept.

Students can be very bright and academically inclined, but when they do not fit in with their peers, they tend to have difficulty.

A student transferred into the school I was at from a local high school; he was a junior. He was a respectful kid who tried to please the people around him; he was looking for a fresh start. The issue we saw was that his past had come with him to our school. The students heard these stories and never really gave him a chance to succeed. Part of his struggle was his disinterest in school, but his biggest obstacle was rejection from his classmates and other students around him. Despite this adversity, he put his head down and worked as hard as he could. By the end of the year though, it was just too much. He ended up failing three courses and transferred back to his old school to finish.

One year later, I ran into this student. The first observation I made was the huge smile on his face, the same smile I saw when he first started attending school. We talked about him and his journey since leaving our school. When I spoke with him, he was in his fifth year taking night classes and was set to graduate at Christmas. He was looking to pursue technical options after completing high school. As an educator, regardless of the journey, these are the stories which keep our passion burning. But as I thought about that conversation, I began to realize this student was completely capable of fulfilling the requirements to graduate from high school, but was not able to because of the environment within our school. After this conversation, I began to look at students within our school who needed a boost to get through tough times and promote a better learning environment for all of our students.

Change is hard. The problem is change does not get easier as we get older. We get comfortable with what we know and branch out from that security; this is when good friends are made. Adults usually become more accepting to new people in their life. Teenagers are a little different in this sense. First impressions play a big role in whether students are going to fit in with their peers and ultimately deciding how many friends they have.

Another important lesson to learn is that the quality of friends is much more important than the quantity. At times, we build many new relationships but struggle to maintain because of the high number. We are in an age in which how many likes we get on a post or picture dictates how many friends we have. But how many of these people will be there when our backs are against the wall? In school, students tend to think the more friends they have, the better their high school experience will be. As we get older and these friendships get tested, we begin to understand the strength is much more substantial than the quantity.

Asking for help

When we ask for help, we show vulnerability. We allow people around us to know we are not able to overcome adversity by ourselves, and we need help to achieve. Those who are successful are able to overcome this vulnerability and rely on people around them to help. Also, those who are truly happy are also those who are able to ask for help during troubled times. Regardless, asking for help is still difficult.

So why is it so hard to ask for help? We grew up in a society that promotes "do it ourselves," When we struggle to "do it ourselves", we are labeled as lazy, unknowledgeable, or sometimes even incompetent. A feeling overcomes us of failure and we struggle to ask for help when we are in need. Another reason why it is hard to ask is that we live in a society where nothing is free, and every act must be compensated. What will I owe this person after the task is completed?

The student who wrote this confession has put his or herself on the line numerous times and came up short. They relied on people to come through and were disappointed by the result. We may receive a sense of vulnerability when we ask for help and that person accomplishes the task, but when we ask for help and that person does not deliver, we become even more self-conscious. When we ask for help, we put our trust in people to help us overcome our problems. When people come up short, we struggle to ask for help the next time we are in a predicament, even though we may need the help to persevere.

This confession makes me think of students who struggle to ask for help. The one time they build up enough courage to ask questions, they either do not receive the information they are looking for or are humiliated for asking a "stupid" question. Our reaction and response we give when people ask for help will dictate the likelihood of them asking for help again. With some people, we only have one chance for them to gain enough confidence to ask for help. Teachers need to understand this when dealing with students. Regardless of how their day has been, student relationships are on the line every time we walk into the classroom.

What prior experiences has this student been involved with that led to giving up? Was someone in their life not helping him or her to get through tough times? Was one of their friends not giving him or her guidance to help them be successful? Was a new student struggling with every aspect of school but could not find the answers he or she was looking for? The need for help is all around us. The concept I try to teach students is they have the ability and power to help and change people's day. When someone is struggling with a problem, being there to help is all some people may need. I am afraid this student is losing faith in the power of people. They have lost faith in people and their ability to help them and will begin to internalize some of their problems. All it takes is one person to step out of his or her way and ask this student if he or she needs anything. We can sum up what people need in two words: support and care. Seems pretty simple, but the impact can be life changing.

Hoping that things will get better

This confession makes me feel sad for this student. When times are tough, we turn to hope to get us through them. This student has prevailed through most of his or her misfortune by hoping; now he or she is starting to lose faith that things will get better.

To students, their life and experiences is all they know. They have not had the opportunity to go off and experience life on their own. Most of their observances have been influenced by their family, both good and bad. This student has hoped for the best throughout his or her life, and conditions have not improved. This sort of mindset can impact development and his or her outlook on achievement throughout life. The foundation of confidence, self-esteem, and self-worth are built at a young age.

When these kids go through a tough childhood and battle adversity throughout, the experiences can set the table for the rest of their life.

These kids do not have the coping mechanisms necessary to deal with some of these issues and it puts them at a disadvantage moving forward.

A good amount of students fight an uphill battle in their daily lives. In some situations, their fortune will not change until they get a fresh start. Continue to fill these people with hope and don't allow them to settle. As an educator, I try to help these students develop a plan to get the fresh start they need. Hope is a powerful thing, and it is the only thing for some.

We can all relate to a time when all the negatives in our life became overwhelming. We worked hard to improve our outlook but had no luck. What did we turn to during this time? We all have activities to keep us occupied or people we spend time with during these times to help us relieve pressure and stress. Our relationship with people and the passion in our life can assist us to explain why something happens. This student lacks the means necessary to help him or her overcome problems in life. Many students are in this situation. The first step they need is to build a solid foundation they can rely on to help them with their issues.

What sort of support systems does this student have in place? How is his or her home life? What are some of the experiences this student has encountered? When a student is struggling in school, those are the first question we ask in education. Most of the times when students struggle, it has something to do with matters outside of the school building.

For a staff meeting icebreaker, I had students write two components they loved about school and had the staff do the same on pieces of paper. I collected their responses and wrote all the answers on the board; students on one side, teachers on the other. What students wrote was incredible. The variety of answers we observed was great, and I had teachers who began to understand the importance and power they obtain. I told the staff about the sad part of this project; while all students had no problem finding two things they enjoyed about school, some students would struggle to write two things they enjoy about home.

How are students supposed to see the light in life when they go home to that sort of environment? This is when people can use their power to change the lives of people around them. In my five years in education, I have seen many parents step up for the well-being of the students. One parent in particular comes to mind in this situation. She and her husband adopted three children and gave them a fresh start. Children all over the world are looking for the same fresh start. She didn't just stop there. Many of her children's friends had troubled home lives and she welcomed them in with open arms. She has been a great role model for not only those students, but also for others who are looking to make a difference. She has been a vital part in two other girls' lives, both of which lack motherly figures. I admire her ability to reach out to those in need and provide them with guidance and strength to overcome the issues they are dealing with.

She is the reason why things will get better for the children in her life.

What is something people misunderstand about you?

Our personalities, attributes, and characteristics tend to be misunderstood in some way, shape, or form. The reason for this is that people do not have all the information needed to fully understand situations in front of them. Human nature allows us to make assumptions about people and what they are going through. What we don't realize is doing this makes overcoming stress and adversity much harder. This is especially true for students in middle school and high school. These students are trying to find their identity and have to deal with judgment and stereotypes along the way. If students did not have to worry about these stresses, they would find their identity much quicker and would not be ashamed of who they have become.

We did not receive as many confessions due to the depth of the prompt, but the ones we did receive were insightful, others were humorous, and some were deflating. Some of the confessions students wrote included the following: my humor, my social anxiety, my feelings toward her, I actually try to lose weight, I am not happy all the time because I deal with hard things that bring me down, I am different than they are, my heart, I do not need to be someone I am not, and your words hurt. After looking at all our confessions, I wonder how these would change if we would do this in an inner-city school or in a different country. Those students are misunderstood, but in what degree and how does that impact them? We talked about this in our sociology class that day. After they left the classroom that day, they thought about the assumptions they make and how they can impact people, even if they do not know those people. The purpose of this project and the class in general is to help students take a step back and look at how they view things around them, and I believe this project did just that.

The seven confessions I chose show the diverse thinking of not only students in our school, but also the students around the nation. These confessions give us an understanding of what the typical student is dealing with behind the scenes. We have students who come to school and struggle staying awake in class or struggle to keep their tempers. If we can take the time to get to know students, problems could be solved before they ever start.

How much I care

Our efforts and level of care is often misunderstood by those around us. The only way people see this is in their actions, which can be tough to do. We show our affection and our love, but often times those acts will go unnoticed. This lack of acknowledgment can lead a person to being misunderstood. When people, especially students, try so hard to show their identity and what they believe in, and the effort is misunderstood, it can be demoralizing. Students try so hard to find their way, and when they are misinterpreted, it can lead to a change in their life's direction.

This is an interesting confession because people care in so many different ways. I look at a passionate person who pours his or her heart and soul into the various aspects he or she is involved with. This individual may struggle to communicate his or her appreciation for loved ones. I then take a look at students who don't say a word in class and struggle to share their emotions throughout the day. These people may be the most compassionate, caring people in the world, but at a glance they feel cold and alone. If we took the time to get to know these students, our misconceptions about them would slowly fade away.

I see this confession play out in education every day. We hear people in education talk about how lazy students are and how they don't care. There are some students who don't care anymore, but they cared at one point.

Something along the way has discouraged these students, and they gave up, they quit caring because they were tired of getting their hopes up only to be let down. These students turn to behavior which gives off the impression that they don't care to protect themselves. For example, a teacher came to me and complained about a sixth grade student who was not able to do third grade material. The teacher stated that whenever they would talk about the material, the student would begin laughing. The teacher believed the student did not care. I know this student; he is a shy and an emotional student who does not want to stick out in front of his friends. I told this teacher that this student cares so much and is so frustrated with his inability to comprehend. He is forced to make a choice: to cry or to laugh. He chooses to laugh to hide is vulnerability and lack of skills to complete the necessary work.

This story is tough to swallow. We judge people on how much they care all the time. When people do not perform up to standard, we automatically think they do not care or are not putting full effort forth. When we do care about something and are accused of not caring, we instantly get frustrated with the situation and tend to shut down. Rather than working through the problem, we shut down because of false accusations based on a lack of facts. This happens with students daily. When we give our best effort and that effort is not reinforced, we tend to lose motivation to improve.

This confession makes me think about relationships we have had throughout our life. When a man asks a woman to enter into the commitment of marriage, he is showing her how much he cares. When we show how much we care and don't receive similar feelings in return, we may struggle to take those risks again. I understand giving is better than receiving, but we all want to receive the same love and acts of kindness we give. We all want to feel needed and appreciated, and that fact drives us to care for the people around us.

When we grow with people, we begin to take what they offer for granted. Most of the time, caring is one of those concepts we take for granted first. We expect to be cared for by those close to us, and when it is not present, we wonder why. I have witnessed when people embrace the importance of caring for one another, they build stronger relationships and live happier lives. They tend to thank one another for being there and acknowledging random acts of kindness. They then are more likely to spot the positive acts their spouse does rather than the negative. Positivity becomes easier to attain when we make a conscious effort to do so. When we spend our time being negative, it is easier to look at events in our life in a negative light.

At the end of the day, we all have many components we care about. Those things we care about are what makes us unique. Also, the way we show compassion makes us unique. Talking about acts of kindness is easy, but actually taking the next step and acting on it is what shows people we do care. We care about their story, well-being, their present, and their future.

My addiction does not define my character

When the word addiction is brought into a conversation, the word instantly changes the course of the discussion. People make assumptions and generalizations about those who have addictions. We tend to see those who have addictions and make judgments about their personality and their character. They are viewed as weak, low-class, undependable, and untruthful. Addiction does not discriminate. It can affect people from all walks of life. This confession forces us to take a step back and look beyond the addiction and truly get to know this person and his or her personality.

We all have challenges and issues we come across in our lives. We have weaknesses that, unfortunately, define us as human beings. When people look at these challenges and issues in our lives, we hope they can put that aside and get to know us for who we really are; this is what this person wants the people around them to do as well. They want them to realize they do have an addiction, but to put that fact aside and leave the judgment out. These assumptions get in the way of many potential friendships and relationships.

Some students battle with addiction each and every day, among battling other circumstances in their life. We turn to addictive means in times of stress because they give us relief. The relief comes in the form of dopamine, a chemical in the brain that provides a sense of happiness. The problem with addiction is we don't receive that initial high ever again. It leads to the chasing of the initial high and gives the user a sense of emptiness. This emptiness may be adding to an individual who is already struggling and will cause psychological problems down the road. We all have different ways we cope with issues in our life, this is just one option some people turn to in time of need. This goes back to getting to know the people around us and knowing some of their backgrounds and experiences.

We make assumptions on people based on what we know and leave out the information that can give reasoning for the actions we are witnessing.

We can help people with their addictions and the problems they are dealing with when we can make connections on a personal level with them. When we take the time to get to know them and show them we care, we can look past what we see on the outside and be able to focus on the characteristics that really matter. This will provide hope and a network of support for these people to help them fight their addiction.

I know a very well-respected man who battled with an addiction to prescription medicine. This individual had surgery on his leg and was prescribed Vicodin, a prescription that helps relieve pain after major surgeries. He lived a normal life, he had a family with a child, and he worked a great job. He really had no problems with his current situation or his upbringing. He was just put in a situation that was a bit too deep and needed the people around him to help him with his addiction.

I don't believe many people knew about his addiction to this medicine, and if they did, how would their perceptions of him change? He is a great guy and would do anything to help his friends and family. He is a trusted and important employee who is dependable and a great role model for students and co-workers. But, some would rather look at the addiction and make assumptions based on that. This is the problem with our society: we often put labels on people, and those labels never fade away. Some folks probably would still look down on this gentleman for an addiction that occurred many years ago. Rather than ridiculing and judging, we could celebrate his courage and strength through the process. We could admire his family and friends for being there for him in time of need. Two ways to look situations always come up in our life, and how we look at them will define our overall success. I strive to look at occurrences in my life, take the positives from them, and build the people around me up. This helps to create a welcoming environment that encourages people to work together to achieve their goals.

I have come to respect those who are able to overcome an addiction. The strength and courage it takes to accomplish this feat is immense. I watched both of my parents quit smoking when I was growing up and have developed a respect of those who were able to stop habits and addictions. It was a long process, but they relied on not only the financial benefits they would receive, but also relied on each other's strength to persevere. If we would use this sort of approach, our problems would not seem insurmountable. In turn, the relationships we have would become stronger as well.

Students across the nation battle with addiction every day. Expectations on students today are at an all-time high, and some turn to addictive means to help cope with the stress and pain. Most who turn to addiction are those who had nowhere else to go for help. They need people in their lives on whom they can depend and help them through troubled times. This confession brought great discussion through our sociology class. Obviously, the first items discussed were drugs, tobacco, alcohol, and gambling. I began to stir the pot a bit. I asked them if pleasing people could be considered an addiction. I had mixed, but very good responses. I then read the definition of addiction, which is the condition of being addicted to a substance, thing, or activity. I then asked them if people sacrifice certain values and what they believe in to try to fit in and please people. Then do they continue to do this and ultimately change who they are just to fit in. The first time we please people on a large scale, we receive a great satisfaction that cannot be matched. We then chase that satisfaction and will never get to that same point. The students agreed that pleasing people could be an addiction.

Addiction may change us to a certain extent, but our character lies within. This student has dealt with judgment because of the addiction and wants to show people his or her true identity. Looking past the addiction and straight to a person's character can help a person overcome their issues. They need to know their character is strong and unique. They need a sense of hope, and that is what we can do for those people. When they receive support, that support becomes the first step to overcoming the addiction.

Student Comment

Sometimes it happens that we strike a person erroneously by our first impression. Sometimes our first interaction with people deals with addictions, and we tend to make judgments, which is not fair.

I am scared, but darn good at hiding it

Being scared can impact the success of an individual. Various objects come into our life that scare us. Do we hide those feelings from the people around us? And if so, why? When we succumb to our fears and show the people around us we are scared, we become afraid of how that will impact us in the future. How will this revealing change our current relationships? How will we be viewed by our peers? How does it change our routine? These are all questions we ask ourselves when we look to reach out to others for help.

People cross our paths every day, and the fear each person has can go unnoticed. Fear may not allow them to put full trust into others. These people may not be open to meeting new people or getting to know their story, but they are looking for someone with whom they can trust to share their fears. We have to be open to all possibilities when we meet new people and begin to build relationships. We need to understand what scares this person and how that impacts the person on a daily basis.

This confession tells me a lot about what this individual thinks of his or her surroundings. When people are comfortable, they tend to share their emotions with the people they trust. They are not as concerned with what people think and trust they will accept them regardless of the confession. When these sort of environments exist, success and development is at an all-time high. Strong leaders and full buy in by all involved create an environment which promotes, honesty, security, comfort, and encouragement.

The biggest problem in education is disconnect of teachers and students. As we get older, we begin to lose sense of what students are going through and how they think. This fact is not our fault as adults, it is just how life works. I asked our class what students have to be afraid of in high school. I was surprised to hear some of the comments they made and how similar they are to what adults fear as well, just in different context. The answers were anywhere from failure, rejection, their future, certain people, and other aspects of their life over which they had no control. This is where we can connect to people, when we take time to get to know their experiences, what makes them happy, what makes them scared, and what their aspirations are.

The gaps created throughout society can be bridged by just taking the time to get to know people and showing them they are cared about.

Students and adults are very much alike when it comes to this confession. We all have fears in this life, whether they are rational or irrational. I look at the life of a students and what they have to be afraid of. Their fear, most times, plays in the hands of the people around them. Family members, friends, and peers have the ability to create situations of high stress and anxiety leading to this fear. For example, an alcoholic father is abusive when he has too many drinks. This can cause stress and fear to this student throughout the day and impact him or her negatively. Family members, friends, and peers also have the opportunity to be the opposite. For example, a friend lives right next door to this student and will keep his window unlocked in case his friend needs a place to stay when his dad gets home. In this situation, this particular individual has no control over the situation and has people around him willing to help.

The student who shared this confession is proud of his or her ability to stay strong through various adversity. School is hard. Students are going through many different situations and most do not have the coping mechanisms necessary to get through some issues. This project gave them the release they deserve. Some of these students just need to hear that they are not alone and many people go through this same feeling every day. They need to know people care for them, and they will get through it together. They have to develop a strong group who they can trust and share that they are scared and need help. This will give them a sense of release and the building of hope and perseverance will begin to develop. The speed of the recovery will depend on those whom with we spend our time. If we have a solid group of people around us, this process will go quite quickly. If we are forced to overcome alone, our process will be interrupted frequently by negativity.

Student Comment

This response is touching because you don't know what this individual really feels inside. If I'm scared, people can tell and they help me through it. This individual can't get help or advice because they show no fear.

I am insecure

We all wish we could change or improve a part in our lives. Those weaknesses or blemishes can create a state of insecurity that can impact the way we think about ourselves and our situations. Our inferiorities can have impact on our mindset if we allow them to. When we have a negative mindset when going through life, we will not be able to receive all the benefits offered. A negative mindset and insecurities put blinders on us, and we may miss the true meaning of the events we experience.

The problem with insecurity is it can spread like wildfire. At times, we take what people say in the wrong context, which leads to large insecurities that may lower our self-esteem and our self-worth. We may become insecure about a little characteristic in our life, which can lead to wide insecurities throughout our life. Minor details can be taken the wrong way and can expand to other aspects of our life as well. People who have insecurities are more prone to allowing adversities become additional insecurities they carry.

Our interaction with people plays a role in what we think of ourselves as well. The problem is that insecure people, often times, do not want people to know they are insecure. They will hear comments that truly hurt them and keep it a secret. This is a huge problem in school. Most students struggle to put the emotional aspect behind what they say; they don't fully understand the detriment they may be inflicting on people with their words. So the insecure student has to make a decision, do they let the people around them know their views and hope their situation improves or do they say nothing and endure the pain? Most times, students will choose to be silent.

I went to school with a student who was a gay. He was one who chose to be quiet for a long period of time to protect himself. I often think about how his school career went. Did he look forward to coming to school? Of what was he afraid? To what did he look forward? I know his insecurities played a role in all of these questions. People would throw out the word gay, homo, and fag, and deep down, that drove his insecurity to an all-time high. I often think about times in the locker room where he would just sit in the corner and not say a word while we all got ready for physical education class. Despite the criticism, he achieved well in school and strived to be a good student. His strength and courage to go through his situation alone is commendable, but I look back and wonder how I could have made it better for him. I think about some of the adversities that I have encountered in my life and how I would deal with those situations without support. He is a better man than me for how he handled the situation.

Insecurity is not always a problem, it can be a good thing as well. Improving ourselves can be motivated by insecurities we may have. For example, if we are insecure about our weight, it can lead us to dieting and working out regularly. In that same sense, insecurity can lead us to make unhealthy decisions as well. People who feel insecure about their weight may struggle to lose the weight initially and later develop an eating disorder.

I think about the students with insecurities and try to link common characteristics with those students. I have noticed some people who lack strong home lives tend to have strong insecurities with self-image and building relationships. They are not receiving the necessary attention and support at home and can tend to believe they are not worthy. In anything in life, when we are not receiving acknowledgment for something we are doing, we tend to ask the question, is it good enough? That is human nature. We then look elsewhere for support, and this can lead to unhealthy relationships with people and things that can take us down the wrong path. This is when we call upon those special people in our life to help us out.

Various aspects in our lives can bring about a feeling of insecurity. When talking to the class, I was again amazed by the similarities between teenagers and adults. The class said they are insecure about their weight, looks, confrontation, knowledge, abilities, and identity. Throughout my short life, I have felt a little overwhelmed about each of these attributes, and I am sure most adults have. When I told the students this, it put us on the same playing field. When people are on the same level, solid relationships are built, and trust develops at a much more rapid pace. People with struggles begin to seem lighter because they realize they are not alone.

I do what I do because the stress in my life

This confession makes me think about what some students could do in their lives with a fresh start. They could leave their baggage at the door and do the things in life they are meant to do. So many times, these children are born with an identity already formed. Labels are already placed on these children before they can even act. We do not live in a feudalistic system, but at times, it feels as though some of these children will struggle to improve their standard of living. With all of the odds against these children at an early age comes stress, and stress tends to stick with these individuals as they grow.

Students are unique. They have wide varieties of personalities that make them who they are. Some of those aspects of their personalities change because of past experiences or present circumstances with which they are dealing. We all have days when we are not our usual self. Students have more of these days because of the situations in their life combined with an increase in hormones.

Challenges we deal with and how we handle them will reveal our character.

The ups and downs are what make us unique, and the way we handle those swings does as well. Internally, we all know what we need to be successful; some need more than others. We know what we need in our life to deal with the challenges ahead, but what makes us who we are is our success in utilizing those tools.

Many students have stress in their lives that carries over to their behavior in school. Most times, there is an underlying reason that causes them to act out. One student I worked with while in college struggled due to the stress in her life. Initially, I thought she was lost and was struggling to find her way back. What I found out after getting to know her was something quite different. This student was in the hospital because of an over-the-counter medication drug overdose. At first glance, it looked like an attention-seeking act. As I continued to get to know this student, I began to understand that she was looking for a way to cope. She told me that her parents were getting a divorce because her mother was going to jail. She needed to know that people in her life cared about her and that regardless of what she was dealing with, that they were still going to be there. She was accustomed to people leaving her in life. She needed stability to help her deal with her stress, but she did not have it. I have not had the opportunity to stay in touch with this student, but her beauty inside was something special, and I pray that one day, she can have confidence in herself.

In any profession, most people who find success are those who work well with others and have an understanding of each person's background and well-being. They are able to make personal connections with various people and use those relationships to help them take the next step. This is especially true for those in education. Students are smart, and they know if the teachers care about their well-being and success. I have been in various schools and identifying the teachers that are successful does not take long. Students talk to those teachers differently, and they are always smiling while at school. We can also spot those people in the service industry who are there for the people they serve. They make us feel like we are important, and they appreciate the opportunity to speak with us. When businesses are able to hire and keep these people within, they will see a rise in productivity, and the environment within the workplace will be favorable.

We all deal with stress differently. Some of us wear our emotions on our sleeves and people around us know we are struggling. Others internalize their stress, and the people around them have no idea that they are dealing with hardship in their lives. Some people struggle when they have any stress in their lives while others strive in pressure situations with high stress. Stress is inevitable. How we deal with that stress may determine our overall happiness. Over the past few years in education, I have also noticed how various people perceive stress in situations. I have seen teachers deal with issues involving minimal stress and make it a big deal. They highlight that little stress and exploit it. These situations tend to drag out and impact more people than they should. I have also witnessed teachers handle high-stress situations well by downplaying the stress and showing people that this problem can be easily fixed.

The stress of a situation is directly correlated with the person in charge. When the person takes care of the issue with ease and shows little distress, the people around that person will be at ease and will look to him or her in times of stress. That is when leaders are developed. People will follow those who make them feel protected and secure. That will also foster a strong working environment where many tasks will get accomplished along the way.

I think about the student who wrote this confession. What stresses does he or she deal with? Who supports this student as he or she is dealing with these stresses? How has this individual witnessed stress being dealt with? Has he or she developed the proper mechanisms to be successful in stressful times? Has this student ever been exposed to a stress free environment? How does this student deal with stress? All of these questions are going to play a role in the life of this student and how he or she handles stress and problems moving forward.

I am not as strong as people think I am

I think about our small sociology class which consisted of seven students and how each one of their personalities vary. Out of just those seven students, a few are very sensitive to the environment around them and show people when they are struggling. Others in our class are neutral, and we don't see them too high or low. I do have one student though who would relate strongly with this confession. She is one who has been through a lot in her life, and she lets no one know it.

I admire her ability to put aside her misfortune and not use it as an excuse for failure. She is not one who will be heard complaining of her situation; she just tries her best to make what she can out of it. I have many questions in regards to her life outside of school. How she is when no one is looking? Does her family see a different side of her that students and teachers do not get to see? Does she feel hiding her pain will help it go away or is she one who sees the light in all scenarios? This is how people become misunderstood. The various personalities and mindsets people carry make it hard to fully understand what they are going through. This student plans to attend college and pursue a degree in elementary education. We need more people like her going into the profession. She sees the good in people and sees the potential each person has.

People hide their true feelings for many reasons; they act stronger than they actually are inside. Some will do this to protect those around them. Others will hide how they feel because they do not want to receive attention. People will also hide their feelings because they feel that showing their emotions to those around them creates a sense of vulnerability. It is hard to let those around us know we have a problem or that we are weak, but it is the first step in helping us overcome.

In other cases, people may have had bad experiences with reaching out when they are in need. When they were weak and vulnerable, they relied on someone else in their lives to provide them strength and support. Sometimes the people we trust come up short and are not able to provide strength we need in certain situations. When this happens, we begin to bottle up our emotions and deal with issues ourselves. This can often lead to some psychological issues such as anxiety, depression, removing ourselves, and even suicidal thoughts.

How are people so good at hiding their true feelings? When we hear of someone whom we know committing suicide, this common statement is made: "I had no idea he or she was struggling." People become experts at hiding problems at an early age. When we are young, we often keep information from our parents and teachers to avoid getting into trouble. When we get into middle school and high school, we begin to hide talents in our life that makes us unique and stand out. When those attributes are revealed, and we hear criticism, we stand strong and pretend the comments don't hurt us; we show people we are stronger than we actually are. We later find out those who are able to embrace what makes them stand out are those who tend to find success later on in life.

If only we could teach students that the talents and characteristics in their lives they are hiding now could end up defining a successful life in the future.

When we keep issues within and struggle with our problems for a long period of time, we begin to see people change. Some of their changes include achievement, goals, dreams, attitudes, and even personality. This is one of the toughest concepts to teach students while they are in school. Students come from various situations and are introduced to numerous experiences that require them to make decisions and overcome adversity. Students handle their situations differently, we just hope, as they move on, they can be successful solving the problems they encounter.

We teach young people that "sticks and stones may break our bones, but words will never hurt us." This saying plays right in the hands of this confession. Sticks and stones will show the damage left behind, but words will allow some people to still feel strong on the outside but will be broken inside. The words of people can play a huge impact on our days, weeks, years, or even lives. The simple words of people can be used to empower, give hope, influence, and motivate. They can also be used to deceive, abuse, exclude, and hurt. Words can help to strengthen people to heights never believed achievable. We can help people to overcome their problems and feel as though they are as strong as they allow others to perceive by simply believing in them.

My feelings toward people

We treat people and their feelings like a book. We tend to take a quick glance and make assumptions on what we think. With a book, we will look at the cover and take a quick look at the synopsis on the back. After that, we make judgments based on what we have seen. All the stories within books provide insight which can help us in life, but we only take the time to look within a certain few. We do this with people and their feelings as well. We take our initial impression and let that dictate how we feel about people before getting to know them. The feelings these people have are based on experiences they have encountered and the memories made in their life. Until we get to know those experiences and get to know the person, we cannot begin to judge people and their feelings.

Past experiences and memories dictate how we build relationships and how we present ourselves. When we have good support and strong networks in our life, we allow people to get to know us; we allow them to access our past and our feelings. The people we let in our lives and let get close to us are those who know our true feelings toward people. They know when we are comfortable in certain situations, they know when we are struggling, and they know our attitudes for the people around us.

This confession instantly makes me think about dating in high school. Students are so conscious about what others think about them and tend to keep their true feelings hidden. They do not want to reveal their attraction to people because it makes them feel vulnerable. This fact can negate many possible relationships as we develop. So when we do show those feelings to the person we like, we get a nervous feeling inside and hope we receive mutual feelings from that individual. When people return this feeling, relationships are built, and experiences are endured. The more success we see with relationships, the more we reach out to people. When those feelings are not returned, we feel somewhat betrayed. We put our hearts on the line and saw no return. This can impact the relationships we build and will also play a role the next time we find someone we are interested in dating.

I remember when I asked Shari, who is now my wife, out for the first time. I was a junior in high school, and she was a sophomore. I remember being so nervous at the time and not knowing why. The concept makes complete sense now. Rejection is one of the hardest feelings to deal with throughout life, no matter how big or small the rejection may be. The rejection can impact us and play a role in how we live our life. It can help us to look at what we need to improve on or it can hurt us by giving us the feeling we are not good enough. I look at how that particular conversation with Shari changed both of our lives forever. Although most conversations will not bear that significance, our daily conversation with those around us can be substantial.

Allowing people to know our feelings puts the ball in their court. When we turn fate over to other people, a sense of discomfort and risk fulfills us. This is when trust and comfort develop. When we turn over the reins to someone else and they come through for us, our trust in people changes. Look at the people who we love and who are trusted in our lives. When we are struggling, those are the ones we look to for guidance. Despite circumstances, they seem to pull through for us and help us out. Relationships are compromised when we begin to lose that feeling. Healthy relationships are hard to come by when our trust cannot be counted on. If we look at people who have gone through divorce, they would say trust was one of the first components to exit their relationship.

I was interested to hear what the class said about this confession. I asked the class about how people can misunderstand their feelings toward people; they gave me a different perspective. A few of the students said they have been in fights with their friends because of situations outside of their control caused them to have a bad day. The class agreed when issues are going on at home, it is tough to come to school and pretend nothing is wrong. The feelings we show on those days can impact our relationships; they often go misunderstood by peers.

When we open up to students, they have a great perspective on life. I would have never thought about some of the ideas discussed this year in sociology. The beautiful part about the sociology class is it changes from year to year. A new year brings new students with completely different views on the world. It also brings complex issues that each student is dealing with in their lives. Students deal with mostly the same problems each year, but with the development of technology and social issues, there is always something new. I go in with the mindset that I am going to learn just as much from my students as they will from me, and we have great discussions. Our feelings were thrown on the table with this project, and when we came across a misunderstanding about one of the topics, we discussed the alternatives and viewpoints from those in the class.

Of what are you most proud?

Pride is a concept associated with all aspects of life. In education alone, pride and lack thereof, plays a dynamic role in the success of students. Students have the ability to use pride to achieve great feats. They also must deal with pride getting in the way of accomplishing their goals. The absence of pride in our lives can lead to underachieving, as well as possibly developing an underlying problem that affects us physically, mentally, and emotionally.

In our society, pride is something that can be earned or achieved. The secret of a positive self-image is finding pride within ourselves. Everyone has characteristics of which to be proud, whether it is a skill, an achievement, strength, or perseverance. The challenge is to use our pride to our advantage. We need to identify the strengths in our life and use them to help us to succeed.

Many people in the world today lack confidence and self-esteem. They fail to look at the good in life and struggle to overcome all the negative encountered. At an early age, we are taught to be humble. This creates a fine line between being arrogant and under appreciating ourselves. This sort of behavior can impact us in all facets of our life. We all endure circumstances that impact us negatively or positively; it is up to us to see where we go from there. Our mindset plays a vital role in this aspect.

In education, pride has a different definition. The only time we really hear the word is when talking about school pride and being proud of the school as a whole. When discussing this with the students, their comments varied. We then began to pick people in class and have the other students address attributes of which they should be proud. Students admitted they didn't see themselves as their classmates saw them. Students get lost in the mix at school. From year to year, students develop and change so much and often times lose themselves. Some of our biggest strengths are ones we do not see but those around us do.

The seven confessions I chose show the diversity of experiences and values within schools today. I was proud of how students looked within themselves. Some of the confessions submitted included the following: my mom, the deer I shot, my family, my classmates, having good friends, I don't know, and my ACT score. The confessions we received were characteristics not easily observed by their peers and that is what made this prompt and project so significant.

My family

When students can see the good in their family, they are putting themselves on a completely different level than most of their peers. Most students are not able to see the blessings they have. In education, we know the importance of support in a student's life. The student who wrote this confession learned from his or her family to appreciate the people that help him or her along the way. When we see the sacrifices people are willing to make for us, we start to notice the good they do as well. Acknowledging family members and their qualities will help to promote positive behavior and create a higher likelihood of it happening again. Parents and teachers use positive reinforcement all the time. When they are seeing good behavior, they acknowledge it and hope to see that behavior more often.

This confession says a lot about the character of this student and their perspective on life. They understand the importance of relationships with their family members and want their family members to succeed. Many people in this world provide support and hope for success on the outside but secretly root against them. Subconsciously, we feel if others have more success than we do, it will make us look bad. Those who are able to overcome this will find much more happiness in their life.

To want the best for people around us, especially at a young age, will help us succeed in our own lives.

This confession is what family is all about. When achievements are accomplished, and goals are met, strong families are the ones who celebrate for each other. They show their appreciation through their support for one another. In education, we see parents who are both supportive and non-supportive. We see parents who are proud of their children's accomplishments and those who don't pay much attention. What astonishes me about this confession is this student takes the time to acknowledge the obstacles his or her family has been through and celebrate accomplishments and the progress that has been made.

When I think about some of the families who I have worked with and what they have overcome, there is great reason to be proud. The resilience they have shown is admirable, and in the end, they appreciate what they have. Families who are proud of their accomplishments work together to move forward to provide a positive environment for growth and support. In schools, we know the students who are exposed to a solid environment at home and those who do not have that luxury. This difference in home life directly links to the struggles in education. We see students at so many levels and have to provide them an education and support to fit the needs of those many different levels.

I asked the class why they were proud of their families and the responses I received varied based on past experiences of each of the students. Some of the responses I heard include the following:

1. My parents went through a divorce and kept their children in mind.

2. We overcame a close family member's death.

3. Our family struggled through an economic hardship.

4. I received continued support and encouragement even though we are on separate continents.

5. Our family is strong despite the move.

The depth of these moments were immense, and we had a small number to pull from. If we asked an entire student body about why they are proud of their families, we would receive some dynamic responses. Sometimes, we don't take the time to appreciate what our families have done for us. Students and their stories have so much to offer the people around them. Their stories can provide a sense of inspiration, pride, appreciation, understanding, and perseverance to the people they encounter every day. If we would just take the time to get to know the people around us, we could learn a great amount about how the world works and how great those around us can be.

My determination

In a world where resistance is all around us, the ability to be determined to follow through proves necessary. The people who see the most success in various aspects of their lives are the ones who show great determination. Some of the most important goals we need to accomplish to be successful are developing strong relationships, being open to change, being able to adapt, being true to ourselves, and setting goals to push us to be the best version of ourselves. Without determination in our lives, we tend to fall short on these needs.

Students come from many different backgrounds and to some, the determination will help to define them. We have all overcome challenges that have made a mark on our identity. The expectations set on us and our ability to meet them also identifies who we are. Often times, more can be learned from our failures we experience than our achievements. We learn how to battle through our problems and deal with the repercussions of failure. Our shortcomings can help strengthen our wills and build us for adversity we will experience in the future. When we are able to succeed without determination and drive, we take for granted what we have and tend to miss small details along the way. Those small details can be strong life lessons that help us to be better people. Student's ability to be determined through the adversity they face will help them to find success not only externally, but also internally as well.

I had a student a few years ago who came to our school from an area school. When meeting with her dad, he said he wants her to just have a good experience because he does not believe she will last long before she drops out. With those sort of expectations, it took her a lot of determination to prevail. She not only enjoyed her experience, but also she exceeded all expectations set for her. She finished on the B honor roll and made many friends with whom she still communicates today. I admire her ability to take advantage of the fresh start presented to her. She came to our school with no expectations and set her own to accomplish. Her determination, if she continues to believe in herself and her abilities, will allow her to find true happiness and success in her life.

People with strong determination often show traits many others do not have. People who use determination to overcome their problems and have worked hard for what they have tend to appreciate the gains they have made. They look at the things they have in their life rather than looking at what others have. Some have also gone through life with their backs against the wall, so they take every situation and make the best out of it. People with determination find the best in all situations and dwell on the positives to keep them moving forward.

Using our determination is much easier said than done, especially for students in middle school and high school. Some do not obtain the willpower needed to follow through with various plans, and others require a support system not in place. Some methods exist that we can use to become more determined to succeed. First, we need to decide what success is and how we achieve it. Success is defined in many different ways, and we need to find what our definition of success is. Next, we need to set personal goals that push us to be better versions of ourselves. Lastly, we need to use our strengths to persevere; our strengths will help us to build our determination. When we are using our strengths to achieve, we are more comfortable, and that leads to a higher success rate.

People can use experiences and situations in their past to play a role in their determination, both positively and negatively. Some people who are struck with misfortune allow that to fuel their determination and to push for a better life, while others allow their past to deteriorate their ability to be determined through challenging times. They use their past as an excuse to settle for average. We need to enjoy what we have in our life and appreciate it, but we cannot settle. Life is ever changing and adaptability plays a large part in the level of our success.

I wish I knew who this student was so I could put a face to the confession. I admire this individual's ability to look in the mirror and give credit to his or herself for accomplishments and strengths. When we are able to appreciate our accomplishments and the road we have taken, the mountains in front of us do not seem as big and the problems we face on a day to day basis do not seem as complex. We begin to gain perspective and not sweat the small issues we come across and focus on the bigger problems that lay ahead of us.

When we discussed this confession in our classroom, we had a mixed review from the students. All of the students in the sociology class came from different backgrounds and had many different challenges in their lives, some more than others. For some students, this discussion allowed them to appreciate the misfortune they overcame and the mistakes they made along the way. For others who have not had much hardship cross their path, they began to realize some of the obstacles their peers had to overcome and developed a sense of respect for them. They began to put themselves in others shoes and how much more difficult daily expectations, like studying and proper sleep, would be. This class, at times, reminded me of the movie *Breakfast Club*. Seven students with very different backgrounds came together and left with an appreciation and understanding for each other.

Student Comment
Determination is something that will get us far in life. It will give us everything we want in this life no matter how high the goal.

My grandpa who served in Vietnam

A few confessions we received throughout this project could be pinpointed to a specific student; this happen to be one of them. This student is one who shows great respect for others. He is one who will drive teacher's nuts because of his lack of interest and sometimes effort. But when he believes in something and is passionate about it, it changes him. He has a strong respect for his grandfather and his service to our country, and his appreciation shows in his daily life. He will likely follow his grandfather's steps and pursue a career in the military.

I see great potential for this young man when he finds something he enjoys and will challenge him. He is extremely loyal to people he trusts and will back it 100 percent once he buys-in. We live in a time that requires us to have numerous stakes in the fire, which does not allow us to put the necessary time and dedication into our endeavors. His confession and the way he lives his life is a testament to living life to the fullest and showing respect for the people he loves.

Respect from this young man started long before he could appreciate his grandpa's past. He started to respect him at an early age for being an excellent grandfather. He thought he could do no wrong and wanted to grow up and be just like him. His grandparents, along with his parents, have taught him respect, appreciation, and kindness. As this student got older, he began to see how much of a hero his grandpa actually was. He respected the sacrifice and commitment his grandpa showed during his time in the service. This is when this student found his love for the military.

In our classroom when this confession came up, we discussed the sacrifice he made and the sacrifice all our armed service members make. We talked about the families and the emotions they go through when a member is in the military. We take for granted the sacrifice and strength of the families of military personnel. They too deserve acknowledgment and support when they are dealing with a deployment. Since these same students took a psychology course with me the first semester, we got into the psychological concepts of war and separation from our loved ones. I wanted the students to understand that, although leaving families was tough, there was an adjustment time when they came back. Military members who come back are often times expected to continue on with their normal lives when they return. Understanding people and their past experiences and taking those into consideration when we meet and talk with them can help them adjust.

Although we may not all have family members and friends who are part of the active military, we all have people in our life who help us and deserve recognition. Some may be public servants who help people in the community while others may have just finished up their GED while working two jobs to support their children. These people need to know their hard work and dedication does not go unnoticed, and when it is our loved ones who show appreciation, we believe our efforts are even more worthwhile. When these people are acknowledged for their accomplishments and their efforts, those efforts are often duplicated.

This grandpa has touched the lives of his grandchildren, and that is something of which to be proud. Isn't that one achievement we strive to accomplish to live a fulfilling life? It goes back to leaving a legacy behind when we go. We all want our family and friends to believe in us and feel a sense of pride along with us. Ultimately, we hope when we leave this earth we leave it a better place for not only our family and friends but also everyone, and this gentleman has done just that.

Having the Lord in my life

We all need people in our life whom we can trust and who can offer us a source of hope. In the world, approximately 84 percent of people identify with some sort of religion. According to an article in the *Huffington Post*, Christians were ranked number one in regards to people who identified, followed by Muslims and "no religion."[4] Regardless if our source is religion, people, places, or things, we need to have hope to live a happy life.

We have seen people change religions and even stop believing because they lost hope. They put their full faith into their religion and were disappointed with the outcome. They lost their faith and looked elsewhere to find hope. We often see this when people are dealing with crisis. They often ask "why me?" or "why would the Lord let this happen?" This can lead to questioning what we believe in and if our time is focused on believing in the wrong things.

When adversity hits, our values, character, and beliefs are tested. We need this adversity in our lives because it forces us to see if our hope and our heart are in the right place. It also shows us how strong we are and where our weaknesses lie. When we get through those situations, our hope and faith strengthens and can change our views. Some students not only lack hope, but also do not have the coping mechanisms to deal with certain situations. Also, these students are dealing with a massive influx of hormones. Those circumstances pose issues for students that can lead to other problems, but these problems become much easier when we find someone or something to trust and instill our hope.

This student has placed his or her trust in the Lord and feels great pride. The Lord has guided this student through the good and the bad, and has pride in the relationship he or she has built.

---

[4] Chin, Jessica. "U.S. Christians Need Religious Liberty Protection More than Muslims: Poll."*HuffPost Canada*, HuffPost, 30 Dec. 2016, www.huffingtonpost.ca/2015/12/30/ap-norc-poll-us-christians-more-than-muslims-need-religious-liberty-protections_n_8894310.html.

Life is easier when we have people to share our successes and support through difficult times. This individual feels the Lord is someone he or she can turn to during times of need or when something needs to be shared. How fortunate is this student that the Lord is someone he or she can put full faith into and relies on Him to prevail?

I heard a story from Brian Hansen, former NFL punter for the New York Jets, during a tour at the FCA building in Sioux Falls, South Dakota. He asked me that if Jesus Christ came to earth and was walking around, would He know who I was. Would He recognize me? Would our conversations connect to prior conversations we had? He then told me if I didn't like the answer to those questions, I need to take a step back and look at what I am doing to build my relationship with Him. Since that day, I have tried to share more about myself with Him so when the day comes, He would recognize me, and we would carry a meaningful conversation.

The next step after talking was Brian was to bring the message to my Fellowship of Christian Athletes (FCA) students. I wanted them to know the relationships we have with not only the Lord, but also the people we hold close to us need maintenance. We need to continually improve our relationships. We also have to ask ourselves will this decision to build our relationship benefit us moving forward. The student who wrote this confession decided that building and maintaining a relationship with the Lord was worthwhile and would lead to a fulfilling life.

Whether we are religious or not, we all need hope. It can come in the form of hope in religion, hope in someone in our life, or hope in something. Those who lose hope tend to get off track and lose focus on their goals and direction of their life. On the contrary, when we see students gain hope in something, it is a great feeling. We see these students come with a different attitude and purpose. In education, that is a victory. We love to instill hope in students and enjoy watching the progress that follows. A student filled with hope is one who will achieve great things in the world.

Student Comment

This is one of my favorite confessions because the Lord helps us all every day and is with us all the time to help us through thick and thin.

Having Thomas in my life, at first I did not want him but now we are buds

Change is hard. Throughout our lives, many people come and go, but very few stay and are impactful. When people or things come into our lives, we have a decision to make, and mindset plays a big role in this decision. Will we welcome them in our life and use them to change us positively, or will we take the change in a negative light? This student, of whom I happen to know the identity, initially looked at the bad in the situation, and that thought changed the way she viewed her baby brother.

I would assume after the change of heart, she regrets some of those initial feelings. She looks at the opportunities she missed because of the negative feelings she felt. We do this frequently in our daily lives: we meet new people and don't take the time to get to know them and don't allow them to play an influence in our life.

We tend to regret opportunities we did not pursue, but the true regret should be the people we did not allow in our lives.

When we look at the relationships that have played the biggest role, not all of them were welcomed with open arms. Life gets in the way at times, and we don't understand the impact of these people. Some may present themselves at the most inopportune times, but making them work can help us succeed down the road. We worry about change and are not open to the opportunities that may exist. I am a big proponent of the common quote "it's not what you know, it is who you know." In some situations, a relationship built is more beneficial than a concept mastered.

I think about this student who wrote this confession and how her relationship changed throughout the years. I wonder if there was a certain event that changed her feelings for her brother. Initially, it is human nature to look at new people in our life from a skeptical standpoint. We enjoy comfort, stability, and routine in our lives. When our routine is thrown off, resistance tends to be the first reaction. Young children enjoy attention from their family members, and now with two other siblings in the house, that means some attention will be taken off of her. For a young girl, that is a hard fact to swallow.

After these kids overcome the initial shock, they begin to connect and build solid relationships. We had a student in our sociology class who was in the same boat. She and her older sister lived a long period of time with just the two of them. When this student was in her late elementary years, their family welcomed a baby boy. During the junior high years, students are dealing with a great amount of change, and hormones begin to race. With all the changes, adding an energetic boy who never stops can be difficult. Life was different, but the girls grew to love the dynamic he added to their family. I asked the student about how life would be without him, and she said she could not imagine. The happiness he has brought to not only her but also her family has been immense.

One aspect of good families I see is that everyone has a role in its success. When times are tough, members of the family use their strengths to help pick up each other. From an outsider looking in, Thomas offers a sense of comic relief to his family. When his parents have had a long day, going home to him and seeing his smiling face can completely turn their day around. Our kids can motivate us to be the best version of ourselves. When they see us, they see the best in us, which is encouraging. The beautiful part about children is their positive outlook on life. We may have struggled through work making mistakes along the way, and we get home and children don't care. They want their parents to be present and care about them. They could care less about not meeting a deadline at work.

This girl who wrote this confession now relies on her brother for relief. They have grown together through the good and the bad. This student struggles with some emotional and social issues at times, and she relies on Thomas for support. Young people in our lives require attention and support to develop properly. What is oftentimes misunderstood is the support these young people provide for us. This confession is a prime example of the joy people bring into our life, regardless of the first impression.

Being clean for over two weeks

Our class had mixed feelings about this confession. For a majority of the population, being clean is something expected of us and is not worthy of pride. Our conversation in sociology did get a little heated as some of the students in our class had this viewpoint, while others knew people who were battling addiction and an achievement like "being clean for over two weeks" would be a milestone. This project allowed people to share their viewpoints and get on the same level in various sociological and psychological concepts. In a world where "me" tends to be top priority, these conversations forced people to look at the other side of the coin.

Students in schools today have addictions they turn to when times are tough. Students are going through various situations in school and their personal lives. When those issues strike, and the support system is not in place, these students need help and they turn to their addiction. They have experienced situations that have shattered their self-esteem and self-image and these activities can act as a release to these students.

The lack of support students receive from their peers and teachers is a result of them not understanding the background and situations of those students. When we get to know these students, and are able to celebrate the small steps they take, the likelihood of continued success is much higher. I receive great satisfaction by building relationships and seeing those relationship benefit someone directly. Whether I give them the support they need, help them to make a decision, or leave them with a smile, it is something I strive to do.

How do individuals get themselves out of their troubles? This student is using an effective way to do so. He or she is celebrating small victories and dwelling on those successes. Without those small victories, the climb to our final goal may be too strenuous. At times, some of these individuals are constantly knocked down with adversity and misfortune. To get out of this trend, we need to acknowledge our triumphs, regardless the size, to see the light. At times, we forget the feeling of success and happiness and find ourselves in a rut. I had someone in my life who couldn't catch a break. In a matter of six months, she was in trouble with the law three times. After the third time, she called and asked for some money to help with some of the fines. She is an important figure in my life, and I could not turn her down. The last statement I made on the phone was that she had a decision to make. She could allow these actions to define her life and let it be the theme for her moving forward, or she could use this to fuel her to make better decisions. The ball was in her court; she was the one who was responsible for the direction she went.

I saw a relationship within a school help a student overcome her challenges immensely. The time our counselor spent with her and her parents helped to bridge the emptiness the student was feeling. In the end, the student felt that someone in the building knew her background and understood her situation; this helped the student to overcome her struggles. This student had a tough school year. She struggled with relationships within the school and dealt with rumors spreading throughout the community. At times of increased anxiety or heat, she would pass out. After this happened a few times, students began to say the behavior was attention seeking. This worried the student and led to even more occurrences. Students obtained a lot of power in this situation. If they would have taken the time to know the situation and not make assumptions, the student would have benefited. Despite the tough time in her life, she has grown from it and is now better for the battle she fought.

This confession reminds me of *Humans of New York*. Brandon Stanton goes out and talks to the various people of New York and shares their stories. I remember reading various stories on addiction and how that has played a role in their lives. The common trait of these individuals who were able to overcome their addictions were the people in their lives who supported them. They relied on people or a religious figure to persevere through hard times. The ones who continue to struggle through addiction are those who may not have people to lean on in their time of need.

Without a ladder, people need help from others when they dig a hole too deep.

Me

A fine line exists between feeling a sense of pride for oneself and being arrogant. This is why people tend to hesitate to appreciate what they have accomplished and let people around them know. This student has done what most struggle to do; take time to reflect on his or her life and celebrate what he or she has done. Reflection time is crucial because it forces us to look at where we spend our time and if that time matches what we value. When we do this, we take the first step to positive change.

I think of some of the students, parents, and teachers I have had the privilege of working with in my career. Some of these people have been through a great deal of misfortune and have a lot to be proud of but tend to hide it. For example, a student I worked with had partial hearing loss and was able to overcome the challenge and receive high grades in all of her classes. Here is the problem with our society and how it promotes a student like this. Society pushes her to appreciate her accomplishments and be proud of the grades she has when actually, she should be proud of the effort and hard work she has put forth. This sort of situation happens a lot. People overcome massive obstacles in their lives but their accomplishments do not merit pride. Their accomplishments help them to attain equilibrium, which is a norm in society.

People tend to grasp the visual attributes but disregard qualities left unseen.

I am proud that this student is able to see the small victories in life and celebrate them. As people get older, these accomplishments turn into expectations, and we do not receive praise and guidance. This is when self-reflection becomes even more important. The problem is, when do we find time to do that? We have jobs, kids, and other commitments that get in the way of this self-reflection. Self-reflection comes in all shapes and

115

sizes; people need varied amounts of it. Most of the time, it is done while performing our hobbies with the people we love. This is why it is important to have hobbies that align with our value.

We need to find attributes within us of which we can be proud. Many social and emotional benefits can be gained by enjoying our accomplishments. Those who find success while using their strengths are able to find a good balance. Being proud of ourselves can lead us to being content and settling for what we have. On the flip side, pride can blind us of the journey ahead. When we use our pride to give us confidence and use it to help others, that confidence can help us become better-rounded.

In education, as well as society, when we lack pride in our endeavors, it often times comes with other social and emotional issues. These issues may lead to depression, anxiety, eating disorders, and can accelerate other issues such as bipolar disorder and suicide. Lack of pride is not always an individual's problem. Many expectations set by others, obstacles along the way, and people we come across who do not wish us to succeed are examples that could bring us down. These challenges will test us. Then we have to decide, will we allow these circumstances to bring us down or use them to fuel us?

When this confession was read, I asked the class of what they are proud. At first it was quiet. I talked about how addressing what we are proud of can come off as arrogance and we are taught to not "brag" at an early age, so to share what we are proud of can often be hard. Then, the students began talking about things they have accomplished, such as athletic and academic achievements. Accomplishments are easy to be proud of because they can be viewed and acknowledged by those around us.

The achievements shared in our sociology class were great, and the students deserve to be proud of themselves. I knew the past of these students and the journey they have taken to get where they are today. These students have dealt with divorce, death, moving, sickness, foster care, abuse, and disabilities and are still striving as students and people. They just needed guidance to appreciate what they have accomplished and that they are worthy of pride. This class period offered a time for self-reflection, and as an educator, I felt humbled to be able to offer that to them. This question allowed them to look in their life and look into others around them and appreciate the strength each one displays on a daily basis.

What do you think about when you are alone?

Many thoughts, dreams, and shortcomings are considered when we are alone. We look at what we have accomplished, what is going on in the present, and what we are looking to achieve. Although some people are extroverts and want to be surrounded by others, we need to take time to think alone and reflect. During this time, we need to assess how we are doing, what we have observed, and how our experiences can strengthen our future. What people don't fully understand is our past experiences play a large role in what we think about when we are alone. What we have perceived often times plays a part in how we perceive situations in the future. Those experiences shed light on the way we think about ourselves and the environment around us.

A little hesitation existed when this prompt was presented to the students. Initially, students' minds were racing. Some confessions submitted were jokes, but the serious ones were powerful. Some of the confessions we received included the following: my life story and how it will unfold, homework, why anybody would hate me, what I did to them, dark chocolate, relationships, self-harm, and why I try to impress everyone.

I chose the seven confessions that show the variety of experiences and thoughts of various students in schools. Some of the depths students explore are remarkable. What I found interesting is the similarities of this list and a list that would comprise of adult answers. As we get older, we still think about the same concepts, but our experiences change the way we view them.

What my life will be like in ten years

This confession is relatable to a good majority of the people who read this book. Looking into the future and wondering what is in store for us can be a driving force in our success. This observation gives us the opportunity to look at what we want, what we are doing, and how we need to change to get there. When we are struggling, looking to the future may give us hope to push forward. Looking forward to the good aspects of our life can help us to overcome the issues we deal with in the present.

I think back when I was in school and how this confession played out for me. The general conception of where I thought my life would be has lined up, but the journey I have taken was completely overlooked. Many instances and people I have met along the way have changed my values and my mindset moving forward. The dreams and aspirations are endless, but the process is often overlooked when we are still adolescents. The little details that often come into play are disregarded when we look into the future. As we begin to grow up and witness a variety of experiences, our outlook on life changes. Our accomplishments help define us, but the people we meet and the experiences we encounter make it special.

This confession lead to the questioning of the students in my room. I asked them where they saw themselves in ten years. What makes this question interesting is it doesn't change a great deal from student to student. At a young age, our backgrounds are very different, but our dreams and aspirations tend to be similar to one another. In society, success has a certain look to it that most adolescents strive to achieve. The common answer we heard in class was with a college degree, having success in a career, and starting a family. These are all great futures after ten years of being removed from high school. What I wanted the students to focus on was what route they were going to take to get there, for it is the route we take that makes our story unique; it is what makes us who we are. As I challenged them, I began to see the wheels turning a bit. Some of them realized their route to what they see as a successful life may be a little more challenging than their peers. With that, their climb will make the destination much more enjoyable.

High school students do not understand the change they will experience in the next ten years. For most, it is hard for them to see in the future because their upbringing is all they have experienced. They have only known one set of friends and believe they will last forever. Until this change occurs, they will not have a full understanding. This project has given these students in this class a quick glance into the future and changed their vision moving forward.

I was interested in one of the answers a student stated in class. She said she would like to be off the grid in ten years. What an interesting vision for a student in high school to have! She said all her life she had expectations and responsibilities, and dreaming of complete freedom helps her through the various situations in her life. These are the conversations that reinforce my decision to go into education. These conversations make students think about their current standing, their future, and the people around them. When this confession was first read, students thought very little about it. When we finished, they had a whole different meaning of their outlook in ten years. The students took a deep look into their lives, their individual journeys they have been on, and their future that lies ahead.

Student Comment
I think about this confession all the time. I wonder, will I be married? Will I have kids? What will I be doing in the professional world? It is exciting and scary at the same time.

Why I am never good enough to hang out with.

Rejection is a common occurrence in one's life. When looking at the relationships in our life, both current and past, we may take the relationships that have faulted somewhat personally. We feel our inferiorities lead to these situations, and that can be hard to accept. But we don't look at how our lives change, our values change, and our interests change as we get older.

As we change, we are introduced to new people who provide different perspective, some good and some bad. The people we spend our time with can be a direct correlation of our personalities and our goals. When we hang out with people who push us to be better people, we often times become better people. When our friends hold us back, we tend to let them do so.

In our life, especially throughout school, friends tend to play a crucial role in our success. We rely on them through thick and thin. What we find out is only a few of our high school friends actually last. A majority of our strong friendships are built after school and throughout adulthood. The reason for this is that we rely on our friends in different ways as we age.

Students have a variety of interests and try to find friends who share those same interests. One of the problems of a small school is friends who share those same interests may be hard to come by. I have had a few students in prior schools who complained about lack of friends and what I would do in their situation. I shared with them that although I had some close friends I still talk with from high school, my friends I talk with the most are those that I met in college and after. I told them I share the same interests with these people, and this helps us to stay in touch. Students need to be able to see past their high school experiences and just because they are struggling now, doesn't mean that is a common trend for them moving forward.

Death

Regardless of how we spend our time and what we do with our life, the idea of death is quite daunting. Something as permanent and unknown as death can leave us pondering the concept. We know people who have passed away, we know people who have been on the verge, and we have seen a great amount on the news, yet it is hard to put ourselves in the situation. Our beliefs and values will give us a foundation of death and what it means while our experiences we have encountered will change our perception.

I watched a TED talk with Ric Elias, a survivor of the plane crash on the Hudson River in 2009. [5] The lessons he learned about himself from his experience can teach us all about how to live a fulfilling life. Everything changes in an instant. When thinking about death, this is absolutely right. Our lasts are our lasts, and we leave the people whom we love wanting more. We take for granted what we have until it is too late. Death is inevitable, but it is our mindset that will impact us moving forward.

The best change we can make to help us through the grieving process is to not take for granted the people close to us and the conversations we have with them. Imagine the conversations that would be had and the relationships that could be built with this sort of behavior.

Elias also mentioned about being upset about little details that did not matter with people who mattered. We see family members not speaking to one another because of minor disagreements. We wait until experiencing adversity or tragedy before we look at these relationships and regret the outcome. Perspective in this situation can be hard to gain and often times

---

[5] Elias, Ric. "3 Things I Learned While My Plane Crashed." TED Talks. TED 2011, Mar. 2011, Long Beach California.

people need an outside source to help them gain perspective; sometimes the source is not pleasant. My uncle passed away tragically of a heart attack. He was a great man and is missed dearly by those close to him. He taught valuable lessons to those who called him dad, uncle, brother, son, and friend. One of the lessons we learned through this tragedy was time is valued by how we spend it, not by the quantity. Any chance we had to meet with family and friends was precious.

Why is it we need to lose someone to understand the true importance they play in our lives? The common saying states we don't know what we have until it is gone; our relationships with people are the best examples. When the people in our life support us, we take that support and use it to help us succeed. When support is common, we have a tendency to take it for granted. Because of his experiences, Ric Elias will take the time to not only appreciate those close to him, but also let them know how important they are.

One of the questions we ask ourselves when we think about death is what would we do with our lives if we knew death was upon us. What sort of experiences would we try to encounter, how would our relationships change with the ones we love, and how would our demeanor change about death.

Elias said he was not scared of death; he was sad. He was sad of the opportunities he would miss and that he was not able to say goodbye. Most people look at death and are overcome by regret. They do not feel they have accomplished all they wanted and now struggle to move on. With that sort of mindset, the concept of death would be a struggle to overcome. We base our lives and how we live them on the standard life expectancy and when we are cut short, we feel cheated of time. This can bring us anger and sadness and will overshadow the experiences we have made, the people whom we have met, and the legacy we have built. Those who are able to overcome the initial shock of death and accept it are those who will find light in such a dark time. The clutter in their life begins to disappear, and they see the big picture.

Things such as bucket lists don't become a priority until we only have so much time left.

Why is it that we have to be faced with such adversity before we live our life to the fullest? Priorities come to the forefront, and we live a life we always wanted, clear of distractions.

We ask a lot of questions about death that are not able to be answered, and that fact leaves us uneasy. Some of the questions we formulate are how our family will respond, what will change, and what people will do after the fact. When speaking with the class about death, there were few stories shared. I explained that we struggle to share those stories because they bring back memories that tend to bring out emotions, and most of us feel insecure about sharing our emotions with others. Our society has built a stigma around showing emotions. That stigma shows we are weak and insecure, so we tend to hide them. After this discussion, the students began opening up about those close to them who have died. They talked about the difficulties they faced dealing with these deaths and what they did to overcome the tragedy. What I found interesting was the way each of them dealt with tragedy. Some of the students wanted to converse with trusted people for support. Others wanted to spend time alone to work through their emotions.

Death is something that impacts the lives of all, but it is our mindset and personality that will ultimately impact our thoughts on the concept. The loss of a person close to us can induce anger because of a life cut short, or it can be a celebration of a life well spent.

Relationships in my life

One lesson I wanted the students to grasp after this sociology project was the importance of relationships in our life. Most of the time when success is encountered, we can relate back to the people with whom we surround ourselves. When we are able to understand the importance of these people and begin to make positive change, success becomes much more achievable.

The fact this student is able to take a step back and analyze the relationships in his or her life will benefit him or her moving forward. Reminiscing about the relationships in our lives and the roles they play can help us to appreciate the little acts they do for us. When we let the people around us know they have played a role in our life and our success, more times than not, support will continue or even increase.

The best conversation our class had about this confession was the friendships these students had at the moment. I told them to look within those relationships and what they receive from them. A healthy relationship offers support, guidance, motivation, and a source of entertainment. I had a few students explain the relationships in their lives and what they were offering. Each student confessed they did have relationships that did not push them to be better versions of themselves. We all have been involved with those types of relationships, and that is fine, but we need to understand time spent with these people will not push us to achieving our goals.

We also talked about why we lose touch with a majority of our high school friends. Many of the students in the class had older brothers and sisters, and they agreed their siblings' best friends were people they met after high school. The reason for this is the responsibility we place on these friends when we get older. We look for more than just entertainment when we are with these friends. Most of the time, the people we surround ourselves with are our support group. We are away from home and need support to be successful, so we rely on our friends. This forces us to spend time with those we can trust, those who support us, and this leads to stronger relationships. Our high school friendships can last, but to be a meaningful relationship, they need to evolve.

After we discussed the students and their friendships, I began to think of relationships that have come and gone. I ask myself questions why some of the relationships I tried so hard to maintain have fallen through. As we get older, we begin to understand that quality plays a much bigger role than quantity in regards to friends. I see students who spend time with very few friends, but the bonds among those friends they have built are strong and can last. I then look at students who have various groups of friends but struggle to make those strong bonds needed as we move forward. The difference between these situations is the substance of these friendships. Often times those people struggle after school to build strong relationships that last because they have never had to do it before.

When our friendships falter, we cannot take it personally; people grow apart. We get so busy with our day-to-day lives and there is not enough time in the day to devote to strengthening all of our friendships. Declining friendships can often times be caused by various life changes, such as having kids or our careers. We also see the change of values playing a role in a declining friendship. When we try to maintain all our friendships, we will stretch ourselves too thin, and this will lead to straining the most important relationships we obtain.

We tend to gravitate to those friends with whom we share common interests; but why? Subconsciously, we enjoy talking to people with little effort. We want to be able to have flowing conversations that take little commitment. When we are able to do this, it means we share interests with them. This can be an issue though. Every relationship takes effort, and conversations need to be meaningful as well. We can compare values and goals and help each other achieve them.

How to make things better for my family

We are not true providers for our family unless we ask ourselves the question "how can I make things better for my family." In the lives of millions around the world, family is what we live for. They are there for us in time of need, they support us through the best times and the worst times, and they push us to be the best we can be. With those circumstances, we will do anything to make conditions better for our family.

A majority of the class first thought the best way to make the lives better for their family was to help financially. We all have roles within our family we need to play, and those roles vary depending on family dynamics and situations. While some students are expected to be kids and enjoy their childhood, others are expected to work a full time job and help pay the bills. This confession can have a completely different meaning depending on which student reads it. But there is much more to this confession than just financial need. Students in our schools witness abuse, neglect, addiction, absence of a family member, and illness. They all have different backgrounds that demand different plans to make matters better for their families.

When everyone is able to fill their roles that the family requires, those families tend to find a little more success. When times are tough, and our families are struggling, we do everything we can to right the ship. We are willing to change everything for those we love. This leads us to stretching ourselves too thin and forgetting our true role within our family. Because of this, relationships within our families become strained. This causes us to take a step back and ask ourselves "Is less more?"

If we spend our time doing less and focusing on it, does it bring us more in the end?

I think of a family I worked with a few years ago. A district member and her husband had two children of their own. At the age of 23, these two were struggling to make ends meet for their family. Situations occurred later, and her two younger siblings no longer had adequate care at home. She knew taking on her two siblings would lead to their family having struggles financially, but she felt she needed to step up to take care of her family. These students may have struggled a bit in school, but their attendance was great, and they received the necessities to be successful. Her loyalty and care for her family should not go noticed. Her willingness to sacrifice the success of her life and her family's lives to provide for her siblings is admirable. She may not realize now, but her actions will give her siblings a chance at a successful life.

I look at this student who wrote this confession and ask myself, what was going on in this student's life? For a student to write this confession, the family must have experienced hardship or loss. This student has shown me his or her ability to look at the needs of the family before evaluating what he or she needs. So many times a student is asked to go well beyond what is expected of a child to contribute to his or her family. On top of that, students are expected to come to school and achieve at a high level. Some of these students, although they go unnoticed, deserve great praise for what they go through each day. Waking up and being present for school is a huge accomplishment for some students.

I asked the students what they have done to help make life better for their family members. The relationships I built with these students throughout this process really showed during conversations like this. Although the class did not have a deep conversation about this topic, I had two students approach me afterwards and share some of the sacrifices they made to help their family get by. With some of the expectations placed on those students to help their family succeed, it is an absolute miracle they show up to school every day. As the conversation continued with these two students, I continued to ask them questions. One of the responses both students shared was that school was a place they could come and feel safe and secure, a place where they had fewer responsibilities and they could be a kid. When students state that they hate coming to school, many other students disagree because they believe school is the best place they can be. If students would take the time to understand what others are going through, they may gain an appreciation for what they have and how easy they have it. It may also give them a greater appreciation for school and what it has to offer its students.

Student Comment
Reading this confession makes me think about the differences between cultures and the importance of family. Family has many different definitions depending on culture.

How I can be happy again

Happiness is a feeling we chase no matter our status. We revolve everything around one day being happy with who we are and who we have become. Sometimes we fall out of happiness because of situations we encounter. When we lose that feeling, it can take a great deal of time to find happiness again. The issue many people, including this student, have witnessed is how negative thoughts build up. Negativity is contagious and can be collected very easily. We are impressionable and the people with whom we spend our time and how we spend our time play a role in how we perceive our surroundings.

Most people who have this feeling can look back and identify when they lost the feeling of happiness. This event was loaded with negativity for the particular individual. Anytime we begin to climb out of the rut we are in, we have emotions come back from that moment. We don't reach out to build new relationships and engage in new experiences because of the fear of being let down. The drop from happiness to sadness hits our emotions much harder than when we are able to build from sadness to happiness. The drop is sudden and takes us by surprise, we are not prepared for what is next. This gives us a feeling of vulnerability, and we struggle through those times.

So how does one overcome negativity? The first step to achieving this is to change our thinking about our past. Rather than dwelling on the negatives of our past, we have to bring the positives to the forefront. We have to change the way we perceive our surroundings initially. We allow our initial reaction to dictate how our surroundings will impact us. The initial response can deter us from opening up and accepting the new people and opportunities.

I think about students whose parents have died. They grow up sharing their successes and troubles with the ones they love. When we rely on that support, and it disappears, an empty feeling takes over us. Everything we encounter from there on reminds us of the people we have lost. There are two feelings we tend to experience when we remember people who have passed. We either are overcome with a sense of loss, and we experience sadness, or we remember what they did for us and appreciate the time they spent with us.

Our sociology class had a discussion about this confession. One of the main objectives in this project was to put ourselves in the shoes of those within the school. Some of these students needed support, comfort, and sympathy, and our job was to realize this and provide. We all have endured the feeling of unhappiness, some more than others. Each person has his or her way of coping with sadness, but until we know each other, we don't know how to help people. One of the major reasons I got into education was to help people. In education, we have the opportunity to change students like these who are struggling and need help to feel happiness again. We have the special opportunity to help people without even realizing it. Saying "hello," or "Can I help you?" can make all the difference in a student's life. I think about the student who handed me the confession about suicide. Did this project save that student's life?

I asked the students what instances have come up in both their life and their friends' lives that have caused them grief. Some of the examples the students shared would be hard to overcome. People say high school is the easiest time of their life, but when faced with adversity, high school can become a nightmare.

When people downplay the problems of others, the hole tends to get dug deeper for those individuals.

To help the people around us, it is important to know what they are going through and help them in any way they need.

What I could have done differently

People who want to improve aspects of their life often have to ask themselves what they could have done differently. Self-reflection is one of the best ways we can learn from our mistakes and move forward. Mistakes are common in life, but how we respond to them makes us unique. It is important to not make the same mistake twice, so retrospection is important, but dwelling can make us struggle to overcome as well.

The problem we have at times is holding onto the past too long and letting it define our future. We look at every aspect of our past experiences and think about how we could have changed to make it better. This does not allow us to let go. Every decision we make is made without confidence in fear of making the wrong decision. We go forth being tentative, which can lead to missed opportunities.

I will never forget what one of the students said about this topic. She said she tries her best to forget the past. She understands she could have done some things differently to change her life, but getting stuck on that fact would inhibit her from being able to move forward. She then said she does not enjoy the present when constantly debating about decisions made in the past. Once she understood this and moved on, her life improved drastically.

There is a lot to learn about life from this student. This is an example of us not giving high school students enough credit. This student has climbed mountains and has fallen many times but refuses to give in. She lives life in the present because it is her only chance of success. This student can inspire many to not dwell on their past. There have been times where this student has allowed her past to bring her down, but the growth I have observed over the years is encouraging. I know with support and guidance, this student will continue to find happiness in her life.

I watched a TED Talk by Thordis Elva and Tom Stranger. During that talk, Elva stated "strive to be the person that you needed when you were a child".[6] So many times we get judged based on the presences of that person in our life. If our society would focus on the growth of a particular person and celebrate the journey, we would see more students succeed. This would allow us to forget about our past and focus on becoming a better person in the future.

This confession comes back to having hope. When adversity hits and we understand the source of the struggle, we tend to not dwell on our past as much. Knowing that things happen for a reason and being able to move on from those events will help us to continue to achieve our goals.

---

[6] Elva, Thordis, and Tom Stranger. "Our Story of Rape and Reconciliation." TedWomen. Oct. 2016.

Describe your life in six words.

In a life full of so many distractions, we are left with six words to define our life. Although coming up with just six words may be hard, it can be a powerful self-reflection. Out of the seven prompts, this question was the one that made the students think the most. The other prompts had given students room to make jokes and come up with some pretty clever responses, but not this one. When we talk about what defines our life, we begin to reminisce about our actions and the events that have occurred. We look at those we have spent our time with and what we have endured together.

Some of the responses we received included the following: "Lies, lonely, hated, conflicted, boring, confusing," "Blessed with the best, but broken," "Chose family, Carpe Diem, Fall, Standup," "Rollercoaster, but I'm enjoying the climb," and "Stay positive even when I'm down." I took pride in knowing students in our school, but this project has shown me there is so much more to learn. This project shows us a valuable lesson that we should never settle with our relationships; we should continue to build new relationships and grow existing ones.

The seven I chose give us a good idea of what high school students are experiencing on a daily basis. These confessions collected show that students are resilient and are excellent at hiding their emotions. They shows the strength of students and how they push on despite their feelings inside. These confessions made me take a step back and look at my job and how I can help students to become better versions of themselves.

Trying to find my way back

Most people in some way, shape, or form have felt the sense of "finding their way back." What we find out throughout life is this confession is a common thought. We endure setbacks and are looking to find our way back to normality.

Students are resilient. They constantly fight battles with school, activities, and at home. As soon as they overcome a problem, a new one seems to arise. When these problems begin to pile up, it becomes harder for them to get back to what seems like a normal life. What they eventually find out is that problems are common and the way we deal with them on a day to day basis will play a direct role in our happiness.

In this confession, they are referring to normal. What this student doesn't understand is that normal has a wide range of definitions depending on the student. For some, trying to find their way back is a huge feat. For others, the idea of normal is the nightmare they are forced to endure. My question, what is this student trying to find their way back from? Has something happened that has shook them? And how has their "funk" affected them physically and emotionally. These questions have to be answered when educators, parents, and friends come across a person struggling. When we are able to answer those questions, we will be able to offer help to overcome the adversity.

When looking at successful people and their journey to the top, a trend is oftentimes observed. Those people tend to do remarkable acts when they are faced with hardship. They have a quick turn around when they make a mistake and do not make the same mistake twice.

When I read this confession, I thought about the students and adults finding their way back from suicidal ideation. This is often a journey that gets underplayed and the individual can relapse. Suicide is a delicate topic and these people need help, guidance, and a strong support system to help them back. What also gets overlooked is the internal battle these people fight. The emotions and thoughts they experienced are hard to overcome, and may never be overcame. From an outsider, one way to help is to understand their situation and appreciate their strength throughout the battle. Letting them know there is support can help them to find their way back.

When we isolate ourselves during times of trouble, we struggle to find our way back. We begin to bottle up the weight of our situation and that will affect us in many aspects of our life. Often times the people who deal with crisis the best are those who use the people around them and the present resources to their advantage.

After the confession was revealed to the class, all of them were able to relate. We discussed the emotions displayed throughout our journey. This confession brought about one of the better lessons through the duration of the project. It showed us that everyone is fighting battles, and most are great at hiding their issues. We may not know what their situations are, but need to apprehend their circumstances and sympathize with them. When we do that, we ease some of the weight people are carrying in their life.

Blessed but it's a struggle sometimes

This confession tells me a lot about the student who wrote it. They understand that despite the struggles they have to endure, they are still blessed. When we adjust our mindset, we begin to embrace the little moments in our life. We tend to see the misfortune of some people and appreciate what we have more. Without this mindset, this student would struggle more during the tough times.

This sort of thinking puts the important people and moments in perspective. We can all struggle with issues, but it is important to remember what is special and how each day we get is a blessing. When we are able to do this, our days become more meaningful and the likelihood of making a difference increases immensely. We begin to see opportunities which lie ahead and take action to improve our circumstances.

During the class discussion, we began to talk about struggles that people have and how they vary. We talked about how one person's struggles and how they perceive them can be very different than other people with those same struggles. Some people tend to take the small problems and magnify them to be almost insurmountable, while others are able to handle them on a small scale. Those who can solve their problems efficiently will be able spend more time and effort on priorities in their life. They won't allow small issues to get in their way of what they want.

We all have struggles, and that struggling can be something which helps define us. The ability to deal with the struggles and overcome them helps us to enjoy the achievements. We struggle to see this concept until we observe a defining moment. I think of someone who is in remission of cancer. The battle they sustain is taxing, but if they are able to overcome cancer, they begin to see life in a different light. Little successes they encounter now become immense accomplishments.

I think about a guy with whom I played ball. He was an easy going guy with a contagious smile. Every time I was with him, I knew memories were going to be made. After battling some pain, doctors diagnosed him with cancer. Despite the diagnosis, he remained optimistic throughout.

When times were dim and unfavorable, he remained strong. After months of battling, the family was informed that they would have to amputate his leg. Again, he took the news with a grain of salt and was just happy to be alive and be there for his family. After a few months of his battle, we had the honor to spend some time together playing softball. Just listening to him talk was a gift. The way he viewed the little details in life was admirable. Things he overlooked before, began to bring him happiness and humility. There is much to learn about how to set our priorities and that we are not always guaranteed another day.

After enduring his struggles, he understands he is blessed with great family, friends, and health. What he realizes that the struggles in our life, at times, help us to understand the beautiful features we are exposed to.

When we have blessings, we look for people with whom to share them. When we have those people, we can share the struggle with them as well. Those people who are truly close to us want to help us overcome our problems and take ownership in our struggle. When the struggle becomes immense, we find those who are with us for the right reasons. The problems we encounter become much more manageable as well.

Depressing and lonely day by day

When we experience loneliness, we feel as though we are in an uphill climb. When we are depressed, we need to reach out to those around us to help us battle back. If loneliness takes over instead, it makes our journey back so much more intimidating. Depression and loneliness change from case to case, and their severity plays a part in how one functions. Loneliness is a hard problem to help people with because it is hard to observe. It is also a hard feeling to help with because it is not easily understood by many people. Some people wonder why they just can't be happy. When people can't relate to the feelings, it is very hard to offer beneficial assistance.

I think about depression and the effects it has on people. I have battled with anxiety in my life, but have found ways to overcome it. Depression impacts people on a different level though. It inserts a sense of doom and getting out of that slump is very hard at times. As depressing feelings set in, we begin to remove ourselves from those in our life, creating an increased sense of loneliness as well.

The problem with depression is that it builds. Depression is not a feeling that plateaus; it usually gets better or worse through time. The people around those who are suffering are either helping or hurting them. Those who have the power to make a difference either are or aren't; there is no in between. With this mindset, people will begin to reach out to more people in need.

When we feel responsible for the misfortune around us, it can push us to do more to help.

So let's put together a hypothetical situation. A student who has been lonely and depressed for a long period of time finds no way out so he or she commits suicide. We look back at our relationship and wonder if we made a difference in his or her life. The problem with this introspection is people often times put themselves in the middle of this question when there really isn't a middle ground. That misconception leads to people not reaching out and helping those in need. They tell themselves that although they didn't help the person, they didn't hurt them either. This sort of thinking will negate us from building strong relationships with those around us.

Many components to this confession exist, and many people play a role. The first concept we need to examine is the background and experiences of those who are struggling. Knowing the depressed person's background can help us to make connections that will help them overcome. The troubling fact is that past experiences people have endured can cause depression. Those past experiences may have been completely out of control of the person as well. They tend to hide their feelings because they are ashamed of what they have experienced. They believe they are protecting themselves, but instead they are distancing themselves.

In education, these sort of thoughts crush us. We want to be there for every student, and we take pride in knowing what our students are going through. The first thought that crossed my mind was my inability to spot this student and help. What sort of signs was this student showing? How could I help them overcome their depression? How long have they been feeling this way? What I have found in my life is the best way to answer those questions comes long before the problem arises. It lies within the relationship we build and the work we have done to maintain them.

Feel like I can do better

This confession pulls me two ways. On one side, I find a student who is pursuing the very best and continues to push to be the best version of his or herself. On the other side, I see a student who thinks whatever he or she does is not good enough and struggles with self-image. I have seen both cases not only in the school setting, but also in the general public. Our backgrounds and experiences can change our perception on this confession and how it plays out.

To be successful, we need to be able to look back and evaluate our actions and how we can improve. As we continue to self-evaluate and gain valuable experience, we tend to take steps to success. When we do not do this, we tend to become comfortable and settle in. Although we want to be comfortable, it can lead us to becoming stagnant.

The alternative to this situation can be taxing on us physically, mentally, and emotionally. When we complete a task, the accomplishment should be something that makes us proud and becomes a stepping stone to greater accomplishments. When we cannot obtain satisfaction, it can lead us to a decrease in the determination we need to improve ourselves.

When we constantly place blame on ourselves for the misfortune we face, we begin to see everything as a flaw. I worked with a teacher who was stuck in this spot. She had been in an abusive relationship for many years. The relationship she was in did not allow her to think she deserved better. Standing up for herself and changing her life took immense strength. Rather than allowing that relationship to define her life, she uses it to fuel her to become a better person.

I respect for her ability to make herself vulnerable again after what she had experienced in her last relationship. She realized she deserves better and acted on it. Despite her experiences, she sees the best in people and offers them positive insight to help them achieve. I have seen her change the lives of her students simply because she finds and expects the best out of them. She has the ability to see the best in people, which has been a strength of hers and has pushed her through the tough years of her life.

This feeling can be associated with many problems we face. Abusive situations, neglect, disappointments, and unreachable expectations are all issues that can make us feel inferior. When we have experienced these occurrences many times, we begin to believe we are the problem. Our self-worth plummets and the time we spend begins to lose value. At this stage, to improve our quality of life, it is important to lean on those who are close to us.

The confession was evaluated by the class and we discussed how this confession is viewed by the general public. I asked them who has done something in their life and wished they could have done better or tried harder; all of the students spoke up. I told them that understanding what it takes to be successful is the first step in improvement. I then asked the students about times in which they tried their best, but felt as though they needed to do better. A majority of the stories shared revolved around athletics and other student activities. Parents have the opportunity to empower their children to be the best they can, but they also have the opportunity to ruin their children's experience with unreachable expectations. The best way to overcome this is to have a set of high goals that push us to do our best and establish those goals with those around us.

I regretted, I decided, I succeeded

This student needs to be the poster child of the ideal mindset that all people need to have. Many people look back on choices they have made and regret them. Regret often times does not allow them to move past and achieve highly. We tend to allow little mistakes to play a large role in our overall happiness and success.

This student was able to grasp that a choice he or she made did not go accordingly and did not align with their values, and they were able to move on. He or she developed a plan and executed. With this sort of mindset, it is not the downfall highlighted, it is the journey and the accomplishment. So many times we struggle to let our misfortunes go and move on. This emphasizes our weaknesses we show rather than using our strengths to our advantage.

Our class broke down this confession. We discussed the process this student went through and the struggles encountered at each stage. The first part "I regretted," drew the most discussion. Some of the decisions students make in high school are made without the consideration of the future. When those decisions are made, it may lead to regret later in life. We talked about some of the decisions we are faced with each day and how those decisions can come back to us. When we are in high school, we do not realize the magnitude of our decisions. In many cases, we learn about the importance of some of those decisions too late.

The second component of this confession "I decided," is often attempted, but it is the follow through that our society struggles with. This part reminds me so much of New Year's resolutions. We all decide to go on a diet, exercise, or cut out desserts. The decision is easy, it is the diligence of the journey that is often overlooked. We take one step in the right direction when we are able to decide on a plan moving forward, but we take five more steps when we are able to carry the plan forward.

The last component of the confession "I succeeded," is a powerful accomplishment. Many people witness accomplishment on a continual basis, it is what they make their successes that advances people. When they are able to appreciate their successes and overcome the regrets, they begin to take notice of the little details in which brings us joy.

Some of the decisions we make play a role in defining us, but it is up to us if we make it a positive or a negative. I shared a story about a guy I knew in college. His parents had him while they were in college. Times were tough and demands of them were high. Nonetheless, they did a great job of raising him. The couple was faced with adversity, went forth with their plans, and succeed. Although many obstacles lied in their way, they focused on overcoming the challenge together and did not allow regrets to bring them down. I respect their courage throughout and respect the job they have done raising their children. Their son is now married and successful and they are two of the happiest people I know. They made the best out of their situation and have found success in many facets of their life.

I have no one to trust

I take this confession and put it into play in my life. I know my life and my journey would get much harder without the people I trust in it.

In a world of turmoil and inconsistency, the misfortune of having no one to trust makes for a hard struggle. Our prior experiences and background play a role in how we trust those around us. If we were raised in a trusting environment, we have a tendency to trust those around us more. When we place our trust in people and are let down, we begin to put our guard up. We learn a lot about the world when we are young. This may prove to be good in some situations and bad in others. Our tendencies can be built at an early age, and when they are raised in a struggling environment, those tendencies can be detrimental. The sad part about students and their situation is they may have people in their life who are worthy of gaining their trust, but their past experiences do not allow them to open up.

To be successful, we need to surround ourselves with people we trust and respect. Those are the people we look to help us when we are in a pinch. They bring out the best in us and push us to be better people. Some of these people have been in our life for many years and others come to us in the most unusual ways. I think of the fragility of relationships and all that goes into making them successful. Our first impressions, the amount of dialogue shared, and both people's backgrounds play a role in the dynamics of a relationships. When one of those components change, it can alter how much trust we place in a person. Trust is a concept that takes years of hard work to maintain, but can be gone in a matter of seconds.

Most people can identify a "go-to person" to whom we look when we are in need of guidance or support. They are the people who, despite the severity of the situation, always have an answer or advice to help us overcome. What oftentimes gets overlooked is the question of why? Why is this person one we can always count on? We forget all the times this person has supported us and helped us overcome adversity.

Why do we allow these people to go on with their days without them knowing their importance?

These people have played a large role in our success and they need to know their importance in our development.

I have had the opportunity to get to know many students throughout my education career. Students open up to me and share about their past and their journey to where they are today. Some of the students I spoke with are remarkable people. Their ability to forget experiences they have encountered and still put themselves out there is remarkable. Some have been abused, neglected, and taken advantage of. I strongly believe good teachers are able to teach the material and the great teachers are those who are able to take the experiences, dreams, and aspirations of the individual students and teach concepts related to classroom material and life lessons.

Only I can hold myself back

With all the experiences endured throughout a person's life, the ability to see that we are the main force in our success is rousing. It is even more impressive that a student is the one who sees this. With this mindset, people tend to not be negative and have high expectations for themselves. They have a strong self-esteem and do not allow the little problems define them. When big problems arise, they have no issues prevailing.

We get so caught up in other people and their actions. We use those people to make excuses for the shortcomings and misfortunes we encounter. Rather than changing what we do, we rest the blame on others. The problem rests in those we spend our time with. When those individuals take their problems and take ownership in them, we begin to do the same with our problems.

The only true control we have in life is not the encounters and actions that occur in our life, but how we perceive them and our plan moving forward. The faster we come to that realization, the easier success will be obtained. There are issues that make our journey much longer and harder, and most of those problems are completely out of our control. When we dwell on them, we begin to lose power over the issues we do have control over.

When we read this student's confession in class, they understood the respect this student deserved. We talked about the misfortunes we have endured and our control over them. Then, a student shared her experience with the class and it changed the entire dynamic. She believed others were also to blame for problems in her life. She read off the experiences she has witnessed in her life and all the people who have played a role in both the good aspects and the bad aspects. No teenager, or person for that matter, should ever have to experience some of the problems this student has endured. The hard reality is that there are many students across the nation who deal with problems like these on a daily basis and are told they are in 100 percent control of their future. What a lot of people don't understand is all people have the opportunity to succeed, some just may have to travel farther to get there.

As a basketball coach, one of the major concepts I wanted to teach was the detriment to pointing fingers. I told my players each year that the only finger that should be pointed is the thumb pointing right back at each athlete. We can only control what we can control, and believing will help us to thrive. We understand that our position in life is impacted by not only ourselves, but also people around us. If we can focus on the things we are in control of, and work hard to overcome, we have done all that we can do to help ourselves succeed. This thought helps put our problems in perspective and helps them to become much less complex.

In education, I think about students who have troubled home lives and situations they must overcome. Some students are dealt a hand that puts them at a huge disadvantage to other students in the school. They are defined by the decisions made by those around them and are left suffering and struggling to be successful. Although we cannot completely fix the lives of those we educate, we can help them to believe in themselves and give them the tools to be able to overcome adversities. We are able to paint a bright picture of the future for them and help them progress along the way.

Chapter 9

What's next?

At this point in our class, we were at information overload. Before we started the project, the students did not look deep into the relationships with the people around them. After the project, the students were overwhelmed with all the information they had learned and wanted to begin to connect the dots. They now looked deeper into their everyday conversations and pushed on to get to know their friends and peers on a different level.

When we finished the project, I asked the students what were some of the most important concepts they learned through the project's entirety. The students talked about many concepts they will remember for the rest of their lives, but five concepts stuck with the class. Those five included the following:

1. Be kind and understanding; you never know what others are going through

After reading the confessions and putting ourselves in the shoes of various students in the school, we now have a different perspective. We can understand why some students struggle to stay awake during class because they slept two hours the night before. We can understand why some students are very short with us because they have trust issues. We can also understand why some students struggle to reach out for help because they have been burned in the past by those they love. Taking the time to show someone we care can make all the difference. Our time can help them overcome problems they are dealing with. Whether a student is struggling with depression or has no one at home who cares for them, our effort and compassion can help them to push through. Most of the time though, we do not understand the importance of kindness until we meet people who are up against tough odds in their lives.

2. We have the power to change people's life. Understanding is the first step in making a difference.

I told the students in the class, and later the school staff in a staff meeting, how occurrences during the day that we don't remember can have a lasting impact on the lives of those around us. We can have a huge impact on people's lives and not realize we are doing anything. If we could grasp our power and take that power into consideration when we converse with people, our relationships will become much stronger.

This statement seems cheesy to some because they think this feat is unachievable in their situation. They believe they are not worthy of changing lives, and therefore do not look around to see when and where they can make a difference. This project turned our students around. When we put power on a pedestal and feel we don't have any, we may not see those around us in need. Making a difference in people's lives is powerful. When we look for opportunities and act on those, we will begin to use our power effectively.

3. Trusting relationships can be one of the most important components in a person's life.

The idea of a trusting relationship is one that holds many different definitions. People who have these relationships in their lives and rely on them for success would struggle mightily if they were absent. To those who do not have the luxury of having trusting relationship, it is a struggle to reach out for help. These people constantly feel as though they are on an island and the only way to get off is to do it themselves.

When we meet new people, it can lead to the start of a trusting relationship that some people are seeking. I am guilty of this. I believe I would push harder to strengthen a relationship if I knew the person was in need of a trusting relationship in their life. We should come with this mindset every time we meet new people. It goes back to not knowing the people around us and having the power to change a person's day. Building relationships is hard and time consuming though. We have numerous expectations that take time and we feel we don't have time for more relationships. But taking that time can have a huge impact on future implications.

4. Students and adults have similar dreams and aspirations, they just may be in different context.

Looking through these confessions and all the confessions we collected was very moving. The one aspect of this project I could not overcome was the similarities I saw in these confessions and the ones I would see if I was polling adults. So many times we knock on the new generations and how they are unequipped to contribute to society. We need to give more credits for their accomplishment and their outlook on life.

I look at a student who put "Save a Life" on the prompt "Before I die I want to….." If I would have reviewed this confession and not know the setting of the project, I would have thought the person who submitted this confession was an adult inspiring to be an EMT or a police officer. When we can appreciate and inspire the dreams and aspirations of others, it pushes them to achieve those dreams. To us their dreams may be silly, but to that specific person, it may be the future they have dreamed of since being a young person. A person's attitude can change for the better or the worse after a conversation. We can fuel people to achieve their dreams or we can be the reason a dream falters.

5. We need to thank those who have made an impact in our life more often.

Why is it we struggle to write a short, meaningful thank you to someone who has played a significant role in our life but we could write a novel on the people and issues in which frustrate us? When we practice being positive, it becomes easier to us. When we practice being negative, we tend to see the negative aspects more often.

A genuine "thank you" reinforces behavior. It shows people their actions are being noticed and appreciated. It makes us feel good that people are taking time out of their day to show us we matter and our actions have made an impact.

I look at the thank you letters I have received in my adult life. I never looked into them much when I was in high school and college, but I have taken a great appreciation for people thanking me for a gift, message, advice, or just helping them. I have kept a many of them and read through them at times when I am searching for my purpose. They help me to push on and continue to strive to help people along the way.

I was very happy with the concepts and messages the students took away from this project. All people have a purpose in life and need guidance and support on their journey to fulfil their purpose. All people are put in situations that make their journey much longer and harder. Although some adversity may seem insurmountable and some situations people are put in may not be fair, success is a possibility. Despite their background, it is people like us who can help them along the way to achieve success and be happy with their lives and what they have accomplished.